Unwrapping the Gifts of Disability

A Mother's Reflections on Raising a Son with Down Syndrome

May you always find the gifts life brings you.

Jadene

JADENE SLOAN RANSDELL

First published by Ultimate World Publishing 2023
Copyright © 2023 Jadene Ransdell

ISBN

Paperback: 978-1-922828-95-8
Ebook: 978-1-922828-96-5

Cover design: Ultimate World Publishing
Layout and typesetting: Ultimate World Publishing
Editors: Marinda Wilkinson, Will Schermerhorn
Cover image license: VikaSuh-Shutterstock.com

Ultimate World Publishing
Diamond Creek,
Victoria Australia 3089
www.writeabook.com.au

Praise for *Unwrapping the Gifts of Disability: A Mother's Reflections on Raising a Son with Down Syndrome*

What a pleasure to read Jadene's series of thank you notes to her son, Matt, who has Down syndrome. She shares heartfelt life stories and explanations regarding their journey learning about and experiencing dreams, strengths, hope, friendship, letting go, and more. She wrote, "I could choose to be sad because Matt faced challenges, or I could choose to celebrate him. I choose celebration!" Thank you, Jadene, for sharing Matt's journey and allowing the readers to celebrate with you. I am grateful for the willingness of families to share their experiences, for it helps me become a better physician for their loved ones with Down syndrome.

Brian Chicoine, MD Medical Director,
Advocate Medical Group Adult Down Syndrome Center

Jadene Ransdell's story was decades in the making, and that gives this book profound wisdom. What a voice! Her words pour out like clear water. Vivid stories propel the narrative. Deeply considered insights light the pages. Her graceful self-reflections, sharing fears and successes with equal honesty, are refreshing, and moving. This book is a testament to courage despite self-doubt, and the power of loving advocacy.

Will Schermerhorn, Blueberry Shoes Productions LLC

Jadene Ransdell has beautifully written a love letter to her son, Matt who has Down syndrome and was later diagnosed with autism and Alzheimer's disease. She offers her insights on the many heartfelt gifts and lessons that came to her while raising Matt. As a trailblazer in advocacy for individuals with disabilities, Jadene pays respect to the historical markers and the tireless efforts of families that laid the groundwork for inclusion and acceptance. On this journey, she inspires the reader to reflect on the gifts in their own life.

Teresa Unnerstall, DS-ASD Consultant, and author of *A New Course: A Mother's Journey Navigating Down Syndrome and Autism*

Unwrapping the Gifts of Disability: A Mother's Reflections on Raising a Son with Down Syndrome reveals the alchemical power of love to transmute deep grief, loss, and suffering and the inner joy and power that emerges from the focus on others. It tells the story of enriched lives through acts of caring, sharing, and building community. Jadene's powerful book offers a clear blueprint of her personal transformation while guiding her readers to step into theirs. This book is a must-read for every parent of a child with a disability.

Paula Petry, PhD., Speaker, Quantum Parenting Coach, and Author of *A Mother's Courage to Awaken — Hope and Inspiration from My Daughter's Journey in the Afterlife*

Firstly, I would like to congratulate Jadene on writing this wonderful book sharing her journey with her son Matt and the beautiful gifts she has received from him. As a mum of a young man who lives with Down syndrome, I have thoroughly enjoyed reading about their story and the gifts Jadene mentions throughout. My son has also given our family many gifts and lessons and I'm sure he will have many more as he grows. Jadene's book is a wonderful read full of beautiful moments and this book will be a great gift for everyone to read. The directions we thought we were heading may have changed when our sons joined our families but the journey we are on is amazing. Congratulations Jadene on a wonderful book that so many will enjoy and learn about things they may not ever have had a chance to learn about without your book.

Julie Fisher, Author, *The Unexpected Journey: Embracing the Beauty of Disability,* and *The Magic Of Inclusion: Give People A Chance And Watch Them Shine*

CONTENTS

DEDICATION

For my husband Joe, who supported me with his love for more than 51 years, and for my sons, Michael and Matt who taught me how to be a loving mom and how to laugh at myself. Without the three of them, there would have been no story to tell.

FOREWORD

I met Jadene Ransdell in 2017, and I knew immediately that her voice and vision would have a powerful impact for the disability community. Raising Matt, her son with Down syndrome, had challenged her to think outside the box and taught her the importance of advocating alongside those whose voice is often not heard, or at least not listened to. Her influence has been the catalyst for much of the work the National Down Syndrome Society (NDSS) does to ensure our adults with Down syndrome and their families have access to important resources to live long healthy lives.

During our first conversation, Jadene shared her idea for a conference where families could join together to better support our adults with Down syndrome. Less than a year later, the first NDSS Adult Summit was held in Washington, D.C. welcoming 300 adults with Down syndrome, family members, and professionals to learn from experts, connect with each other, and build a community focused on the specific needs of our loved ones in their adult years. Since then, NDSS has held

Adult Summit events in person and online, and Jadene's idea has had a positive impact on more than a thousand individuals around the world.

Since our first conversation, Jadene has lovingly shared her ideas, expertise, and friendship with me, with NDSS, and throughout the disability community. She has challenged us to think bigger and reflect on how we can share stories and drive advocacy that includes every voice and every experience across our community. Her personal experience with her son, Matt, made her the advocate she is today. But she has also been shaped by the many families she has connected with and supported over the years. Her tireless advocacy and attention often focus on those that have felt (and been) forgotten, and her conviction opens our eyes to fully understand that supporting individuals with Down syndrome means embracing the full diversity of our community. A few years ago, Jadene and I met to discuss the topic of employment for adults with Down syndrome. She shared Matt's story about volunteering at a local VA hospital and how life-changing that opportunity was for him. Matt took pride in this job and loved working with the patients. Hearing this story shifted my perception of what meaningful employment looks like for each person—how important it is to feel valued and that you have a place to belong.

I frequently reflect on the impact Jadene and Matt's story has had on my life and the work I do in pursuing NDSS' mission and vision. She has paved the path for families like mine and so many others that will continue to benefit from her advocacy for decades. I know I speak for all of NDSS—and for the Down syndrome community—when I say that I am grateful for Jadene's fight and for her ability to advocate through the powerful stories she tells. She is a voice for a community that deserves a beautiful life. I am proud of my friend and the way she is making this world a better place for people with Down syndrome like her son and mine.

Kandi Pickard, President and CEO,
National Down Syndrome Society

LOOKING BACK
TO LOOK FORWARD

Thank you for choosing this book. Before I reveal the gifts I have for you, let me take you on a little trip through time, back to where our story began. As you turn these pages, imagine that the first messages to me were of no hope. I was told everything that my new baby would never be able to do, like feed himself, use the toilet independently, or live in a group home. I was told I could not expect any of the milestones that our first son had accomplished.

As Matt has grown, a wide spectrum of abilities is now seen in children and adults with Down syndrome. Matt is not alone in the challenges he faces with Down syndrome and his additional diagnoses. And, for those who are able, there are more opportunities available. Today we see young people with Down syndrome living very full lives. Some are powerful athletes, competing in marathons and setting swimming records. Some have successful businesses providing consumers with delicious food, beverages, and socks to keep their feet warm. I know a fellow who is beginning a career as a fashion designer, a woman who lobbies Congress, a young man who has written a book about his life, and several young people attending college. I have a friend whose son with Down syndrome is married. We have greater expectations for our babies, our children, and our young people with Down syndrome than ever before. And those expectations, rightfully, increase each year.

The story you are about to read tells of the power of one little boy to help his mother push through the barriers imposed by his doctors, his teachers, his community. It took a long time for me to find the gifts Matt had brought to my life and that's why I wanted to tell this story. We all face difficult times and we all can find hope and gifts in those difficulties.

Please note that I use the terminology that was prevalent when Matt was born and a young child.

DEAR READER: AN INVITATION TO A CELEBRATION

Dear Reader,

Today, I invite you to a celebration. Think of it as a party with lots of beautifully wrapped presents scattered around the room. And you, dear reader, get to open them with me.

The gifts have come to me from my son Matt. He has the sweetest soul and loves unconditionally. His blonde hair and blue eyes, I like to think, reflect the visible connection he has to me. His small stature disguises just how big his heart is. That becomes evident, though, in the power of his hugs—if you've been hugged by Matt you know that life will now be good. He is a simple man, with few material needs other than a milkshake at night, and cat toys on sticks. He loves for his momma to sing his favorite songs and doesn't even mind that she can't carry a tune. To be loved by Matt has been one of life's greatest blessings, for sure.

Little did I know when Matt was born how his mere existence would have such a profound and positive effect on my life. Looking back at our life together I can say without a doubt that there were lessons in the pain, joys beyond words, days and weeks filled with anxiety, and a lifetime of surprises.

Parents of children and adults with disabilities face society's pressures and demands; yet each of our stories is unique. We must also face the challenges of raising, caring for, and supporting a child with a disability. Many variables influence how we cope and how we face disability in our own family. Parents can feel vulnerable and still show their strength. It's a paradox of parenting under challenge. The magnitude of stressful experiences fluctuates, and how we respond to them, even in the same day, varies. But these experiences are the exact things from which we can learn and grow.

Years ago, I wrote and delivered training programs for parents and professionals. Some of those workshops focused on the grieving process that families went through when they learned of their child's disability. I knew that well. The night I learned that my baby boy was born with an intellectual disability and would never have the life I had dreamed he would, I grieved for the life that was not to be. Sadness and disappointment filled my days. I thought I would never smile again.

And that memory soaked into the trainings I delivered. After one session when Matt was a young teen, I began to think a lot about my life with him. I wondered if I was painting the picture a bit too darkly, focusing too much on the grief. As I thought about my life, I realized that I didn't spend my days grieving. There were lengthy periods packed full of joy and gratitude, and most were overflowing with the ordinary tasks of living life every day. Days and weeks were filled with laundry, grocery shopping, cleaning, running errands, and preparing family meals. Hours were spent playing with my boys, filling the air with laughter, and creating wonderful memories. It was then that I questioned why no one ever spoke about the positive, uplifting aspects of raising a child with a disability.

I began thinking of all the wonderful experiences I had because my son has Down syndrome. Little did I know when the pediatrician told me of Matt's disability that my life would be better than I could have ever imagined. The journey hasn't been easy, but it was certainly worth the effort.

Family needs can shape the way we think about the world. When disability is part of our life, it touches everyone in a family, and close friends as well. The night I got Matt's diagnosis felt like the worst night of my life. Over the years Matt had more labels added. He has received diagnoses of Autism, Apraxia (muscle control problems causing difficulty forming sounds), nonverbal Tourette syndrome, obsessive compulsive disorder (OCD), and more recently, Alzheimer's disease. When doors were closed to us, I found that there was usually a new door opened. Occasionally the door was only slightly ajar—but I learned to squeeze through whatever gap I found so I could move on. Those additional diagnoses certainly added challenges for Matt, and sometimes I felt like we didn't fit in anywhere. Those were the times I worked harder to make sense of our life. I'm so glad I did.

We are ordinary people with ordinary resources available to us. Life is not fair, and situations over which we have no control affect us all. Strength lies in the know-how and desire to face and solve problems. Each of us has the capacity to survive adversities and bitter disappointments. We have a wellspring of strength that lies untapped until we are faced with a situation that bursts it into the open. The good news is we can learn to control our responses to challenging circumstances and lessen their negative impact on us.

The universal role of families is to nurture each other—especially our children. It can be a difficult, yet joyous job. When a child has a lifelong disability, all family members are called on to work together. Through the extra efforts, we develop a capacity to face more intense experiences of pleasure as well as pain.

When I started this journey, the words that described my life included disappointment, anger, fear, loneliness, frustration, unworthiness, and sadness. There were times I didn't believe that I would ever use other descriptors. Sometimes the pain was unbearable; often I felt like a failure. Fortunately, I found people and circumstances that showed me a different way.

I have learned to face my fears, to jump into the things I would have rather avoided. I have learned that disappointment is temporary, and that the hard times do not last forever. I have even learned to recognize how my ancestors imprinted my soul with a strength hidden deep within. I've found that life is wrapped in many layers, and that when I let other hearts hold me close I can do wonderful things.

As I write this welcome to you, my dear reader, I am about to celebrate my 75th birthday. I see myself as an elder now; a woman whose journey to gain wisdom has finally brought me to an appreciation of self. I have been led to authoring this book so that I could share with you what has taken me a lifetime to acknowledge: *The hardest part of raising a child with a disability was not his disability. The most difficult path on my journey was recognizing my own strength and my worthiness.* It has taken most of my years to appreciate myself enough to know I have something within me that has value. Equally crucial, I have learned that it is important that I take time to care for myself as I so lovingly care for everyone around me.

So let's get back to those gifts. Although a few of the gifts could have been expected, many of them came to me as complete surprises. If I can leave you with one consideration, I want you to recognize that there are many gifts presented to us when disability moves into our home. I hope to impart to you some of the wonders that I have found by sharing life with my son.

As we unwrap each present, join me as I share the journey I've been on, learning about these valuable treasures. Along the way, I hope you can look at your journey—and apply some of the wisdom I've gained as you receive your own gifts.

The best is already inside you. And you, dear reader, must know that you have the power to find goodness where others may be unable to see it. You, too, can begin with heartbreak and find happy endings. I hope that you will find the surprises as delightful as I have. Come on, the gifts are waiting!

In gratitude and respect,
Jadene (AKA Matt's Momma)

DEAR MATT: YOUR STAR, MY BLESSING

Dear Matt,

Sometimes I find myself looking at the sky when I think about your life. The night sky has holes punched with light, thousands of tiny sparkling little spaces. There are no clouds to hide the specks of brilliance that I see. I must confess I was never good at finding that lion or the

dippers—even the big one. Everywhere I look, I see all these lights shining down on me. I have learned that some are stars; some are planets. It doesn't matter to me what they are. To me, they are all the gifts that you have brought to my life—more than I will ever be able to count or measure.

When I look up at the night sky, I see some stars shining more brightly than others. Does that make them more important? Not at all. Every spot of light in the black sky is there for a reason and is part of something larger than itself.

Some people thought you shouldn't have been born. Some think you are worth less than a person who is making scientific discoveries. I feel sorry for those people. They seem to not realize the sense of wonder and excitement that you find in simple things—like a helicopter flying over your head. They cannot taste the sweetness of the love you have for your nephews Aiden and Cody, and all the people who are important to you. They do not see the way you heal a broken veteran's soul. They cannot hear what you say without using words.

You, my dear Matt, have been a creator of starlight throughout your life. Every twinkle is a gift to me and anyone whose heart is open.

There have been times when clouds tried to hide your star. During those periods of your biggest and hardest challenges, the clouds were very dark, and joined with shattering claps of thunder. There were times I wondered if those storms would ever clear. Just when I would be ready to give up, you would blow those storm clouds away— and, once again, there you were with your star shining brightly. When you were in school you had many days that were hard for you. Most people didn't understand you. You had angry outbursts and times you hurt yourself because you were frustrated. My heart ached while you struggled. In time, you somehow managed to let go of the troubles and just smile. I still don't know how you did that, but I'm glad you always found your way back to us.

You have showered me with gifts not found in any store. You have given me more love than I ever knew was possible. Without speaking, you have been a great teacher. You have taught me lessons I didn't realize I needed to learn.

And now, my sweet boy, something may be trying to snuff out your star. Your doctor has told me that you have Alzheimer's. I'm not sure this is accurate, but I find comfort in the fact that you do not know what that means. I think this is a gift to you because you don't have to worry about it. Just know that I am not ready for your light to go out. I promise you I will do everything in my power to keep your star glowing. I share your teachings and your gifts with others so that your illumination will burn brightly for many, many years.

For all you have blessed me with, I now give you thanks. I start with this. Thank you, Matt, for the life you have shared with me. I may not have recognized your gifts when you presented them, but I have had a long time to open them, inspect them, and see the value of each through the lens of your life. Always know—in your heart and soul—I am among those who love you deeply; your life is a gift to many and is significant. I will love you for all eternity.

Love,
Momma

A GIFT OF DREAMS

Dear Matt,

Throughout your life, you have taught me how to dream new dreams, reshaping and rediscovering hope for what life can be after my dreams for you fell apart.

As a teenage girl, I had dreams for my future. They were like the dreams of many young girls growing up in the sixties—marriage, a home of our own, children, and pets. In time, all those dreams did come true. For a while, I was certain that everything I had ever wanted would be mine. The first memory I have of changing the direction of my dreams was the moment you were born, and I realized that we would name you Matthew instead of Melanie. I've reframed dreams several times since then. Sharing life with you has helped me learn that it is possible to change my visions for the future.

As you grew, I sometimes had to adjust the dreams I created for you—for your life. I always hoped that you would have a happy life filled with meaning. You, my beloved son, have fulfilled that hope, and by doing so, I pray you can see the significance of your life.

Thank you, Matt for teaching me that dreams can be changed and that new dreams can be just as wonderful as the original ones.

Love,
Momma

A Gift of Dreams

"A dream is a wish your heart makes."

Walt Disney,
Animator and Film Producer

When I was a young girl growing up in Iowa, my life's fantasy was to one day marry my knight in shining armor and have two children (a boy first and a girl two years later—the boy would be named Michael). Together, we would live in a home of our own, have a dog in the backyard, and roses adorning the front of our house. I would spend my days with my children and bake apple pies and fresh bread.

My life would be just like Ozzie and Harriett's. They were a real couple who had a television show when I was a teenager. They portrayed a loving family where the dad (Ozzie) went off to work each morning and the mom (Harriett) baked cookies and pies.

Jadene and Joe just after they were married. February 28, 1970, Satellite Beach, Florida

Harriet always had just the right amount of advice and love for her sons, David and Ricky. They were always happy and worked out every problem in those thirty-minute episodes. Ah, the "Ozzie and Harriet" life—that was for me!

And my fantasies did come true, after I moved from Iowa to Florida. I met and married the man of my dreams, Joe Ransdell, who, with only a little prompting, remembered to put his dirty socks and jeans into the hamper—before I did the laundry. We had two children, Michael first, and then Matt. We had two dogs in the fenced backyard, and roses lined the front walkway of our little three-bedroom home. And the apple pies I made for Joe were the best he had ever tasted; at least that's what he told me.

Every mother-to-be delights in thoughts of the beautiful, sweet-smelling, cuddly baby she will joyously bring into the world in just nine short months. I was no exception; when I was pregnant with Michael, I felt healthy and was unbelievably happy. As I waited for his arrival, I readied our tiny home. My dad had brought me the crib that my sister, Jaren, and I had used. I was happy to have the same crib that had inspired dreams of my future babies. I painted it green, made curtains for the single window, and found adorable baby animal prints to hang on the walls in the bedroom that would soon be a nursery.

On the exact date he was due, after what seemed to be an endless labor, Michael entered the world fat, pink, and perfect. It seems that, as many expectant mothers do, I had worried needlessly for months about giving birth to a child with a disability. The days in the hospital seemed to drag on. Although Joe was allowed to be with me during my labor, he was not allowed in the delivery room and could not be with me after the birth, except during the specified visiting hours. We were rarely apart so it was hard being alone, especially the first afternoon following Michael's birth when Joe didn't return. As visiting hours went by, I lay in the bed, searching the hallway each time I heard footsteps. My mind began going in crazy places and soon I had convinced myself that Joe didn't want to be a father and had left me. Ten minutes before the end of visiting hours, he walked in with our best friend, Michael Stafford. Michael quickly excused himself when I burst into tears and Joe frantically tried to tell me about the new car he had just bought us—the one with a faulty gas gauge that caused him to run out of gas and be late arriving. He smothered me in kisses and life was back on track.

Life Was Unfolding Just as I Had Thought

Michael was the baby of my dreams. He slept through the night at six weeks old. He was always in a good mood, smiling and laughing easily. He was a beautiful child with the prettiest red hair that drew comments from everyone who saw him. At eighteen months old he entered the terrible twos, and I was challenged to deal with his baby defiance. Even so, we were a happy little family, and I was ready to let it grow.

When Michael was almost two years old, I was excited when I called my dad, who lived in Iowa, to share the news that a new baby would join our family. He was amazed at how well I had planned my life, and, frankly, I was a bit shocked that life was unfolding just as I had thought it would.

Two weeks before my second baby was due, I began having contractions shortly after midnight that continued for several hours, growing in strength while the time between them shortened. Quietly, I paced a path from the bedroom, past Michael's room, and the doorway to the nursery, down the hallway, through the living room and back—stopping long enough to breathe through the pain as each contraction reached its crescendo. Soon, they were ten minutes apart and I realized that they were the real thing. It was time to put the delivery plan into motion. First, I peeked in on my little boy, sleeping soundly in his bed. He looked so tiny snuggled into his pillow, with one leg tangled in his favorite blanket, and his little body squished against the bed rail we had in place to keep him from falling out. With tear-filled eyes, I bent over and gave this small child a soft, lingering kiss on the top of his head. Tiptoeing out of his room, I made my way to the kitchen where I carefully lifted the receiver from the yellow wall phone and dialed.

"Hello?" my friend and neighbor sounded confused (remember, this is long before we had phones that identified who is calling, and it was three o'clock in the morning).

"Vita, it's Deenie," I said. "Can you come over and stay with Michael? It's time for me to get to the hospital."

Within five minutes, Vita tapped lightly on our front door. I had awakened Joe and he was just walking down the hallway, not yet alert. Vita and I discussed the rest of the delivery plan. I made sure she had my friend Bobbie Ratajczak's telephone number

so she could be called to take over with Michael around 9 a.m., and then it was time to go. The tears flowed again, as I stood by the front door and Vita hugged me goodbye.

"Are you scared?" she asked me.

I wasn't sure where the tears came from. I knew that when I returned, I would bring a baby with me that would make Michael a big brother. He had been my baby for more than two years, and life was about to be so different for all of us. I knew I was excited too, because soon I would have the little girl of whom I had been dreaming.

The images I had during my pregnancy were of lacy pink dresses, polka dot hair bows, ballet slippers, and long, flowing prom gowns. In the seventies, when I had my babies, there were no gender-reveal parties. So, right up until the moment of birth I did not know if I was getting the girl of my dreams. My labor went much more quickly than it had with Michael. I was given drugs that dulled the pain and confused me a little, so when the nurses roused me to tell me that my baby was here, my brain thought that someone had brought an infant to my front door.

A Dream Changed

I don't know what transpired in the delivery room, but my hazy memories of that morning bring back the questions and answers with the nurse. "Jadene, your baby is here, do you know what you had?"

She must have had a short memory and was a bit argumentative because when I responded, "Yes, I had a girl," she would ask the

25

question again. I wondered why she felt the need to correct me and to insist that I had given birth to another boy. Eventually, I was taken to my hospital room and slept much of the day.

When I woke, I realized that I had been wrong. I was only slightly saddened when I acknowledged that we would call the baby Matthew and not Melanie. (When Matthew was in Kindergarten, I realized that it would be easier for him to say and print his name if it was shortened to Matt—and that is how I will refer to him from here forward.)

As when Michael was born, Joe could only be with me for short periods in the afternoons and evenings. So, I spent the days lying in the hospital bed and thinking of our future—of Matt and Michael playing with their little cars and trucks in the sandbox their daddy had built in the backyard. In my mind, I even found the perfect spaces to park their two bicycles, the ones on which they would explore the world. I could see my boys, alongside their dad, working on car engines in the driveway. I saw Michael and Matt as each other's best friend. They would double-date to the prom and be the best man at each other's weddings.

Two days after delivery, I was missing Michael and getting anxious to go home. That afternoon I spoke with him on the phone and promised I would bring his little brother to him the next morning. Due to final exams at the junior college where Joe was taking courses, he was unable to come to the hospital that day. He called to tell me my friend Bobbie would be coming that evening to visit and would bring clothes for me to wear home, and some little things for Matt, as well.

Dreams Shattered

During the visiting hours that evening, Dr. Kenaston, our pediatrician, came in and asked if Joe was coming to see me. I thought it strange for him to be at the hospital after hours but guessed that a baby had just been born. I respected this doctor very much and was glad to be able to introduce Jaren, my

Author's note: *I use the terms that were prevalent during the time Matt was born and started school and I recognize that those terms are no longer accepted or considered respectful. They are included here to illustrate the perceptions at Matt's birth and when he was small.*

sister, and Bobbie to him. When he left, the three of us walked to the nursery to see Matt. As we were standing by the window, a nurse came up and informed us that my friends would have to leave. "I didn't hear the bell announcing the end of visiting hours, I'm sorry," I said to her. After telling Bobbie and Jaren goodbye, I climbed back in bed, knowing the baby would be brought to me soon.

It wasn't long before the doctor came back into my room and stood at the end of my bed. "May I borrow you?" he asked.

"Sure!" I replied, feeling quite happy because in a few short hours, I would be taking my second son home. As we walked down the cold, brightly lit hallway towards the nursery, I noticed how incredibly quiet it was. I wondered to myself if there was something wrong and I tried to figure out what it could be. I immediately assumed it had to do with Matt's blood as I am RH negative. And then I remembered that Matt's blood was also negative so there shouldn't have been a question of compatibility.

27

But it was the only possible thing I could think of. As we walked together down the hall, I asked, in a voice I could hardly make, "We've got a problem, don't we?"

"Yes, we do," he said.

Although the distance from my room to the empty room where he took me was just a few doors, that walk seemed to take forever. "Please wait here while I get Matt's chart," he said once we were inside. He left me alone with my thoughts and my rising fears. The room looked just like the one I had left—two single hospital beds, bedside tables, overhead and over-the-bed lights, and pretty pictures on the walls. It was exactly the same, yet this one felt cold and cave-like.

My mind was racing, trying to figure out just what it was that the doctor was going to say. Panic was building as I started to realize that soon I was going to hear some really unwelcome news. I didn't want to be alone. My sister had just left; why did they make her leave? If it was bad, why hadn't he asked Joe to come to the hospital? So many questions tumbled through my head. When Dr. Kenaston returned, he opened the chart and began talking.

"Perhaps you've noticed that Matt's eyes are slanted and have what we call Brushfield spots—and he has very small ears." Of course, Joe and I had seen those things—we had even joked about them—but those features had not concerned us.

"He also has a large gap between his big toe and his second toe," the doctor continued, "and a line going straight across the palms of his hands."

And so it was, that all alone, with no one to tell me it was going to be OK, the doctor finally said that all the conditions he had observed led him to conclude that Matt was "Mongoloid." He used the term that was common in 1974, but we know the condition today as Down syndrome.

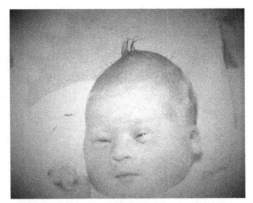

Nursery photo of Matthew Jaren Ransdell. July 30, 1974, Wuesthoff Hospital, Rockledge, Florida

I didn't hear much after that. My dreams shattered. All the dreams I had for my baby's future were dissolving, one by one, into a dark hole that was growing inside me. I fell back onto the pillows of the bed I was sitting on. My head was swimming, and my tears were flowing.

I couldn't believe my ears. I knew what it meant—RETARDED! My mind flashed back to when, shortly after I graduated from high school, I taught a young girl with Down syndrome in a preschool class at our church. She was a cute, quiet child with long brown hair, and because she was seven years old, she was much bigger than the three- and four-year-old children I was teaching. Her parents brought her to Sunday School only a couple of times. When she was there I was scared because I had no idea how to talk to her, or how to include her in my class. I took lots of deep breaths and said a few prayers because I felt unprepared to teach her.

That same scared feeling was back as I thought about me with my baby. I felt unprepared to be Matt's mom.

29

Quite upset, and crying uncontrollably, I remember little more of what was said to me. The doctor was very apologetic for telling me without Joe being present. He comforted me as best he could; I can still see his face, full of concern and caring. I felt sorry for him because he had to tell me about this tragedy. I was sure he must have felt awful.

When I had more control of myself, he went on, "I've already done an X-ray of his pelvis and it shows the wide flange that is present in babies with this diagnosis. The only positive proof of Mongolism is a chromosome study, taken from a blood sample. It's extremely complicated to run and expensive."

I gave my permission for the test, but I knew he was sure of his diagnosis. Although I didn't like what I had just heard, I trusted our doctor. If he and the two pediatricians he had consulted believed it, then so did I.

Dr. Kenaston left me to call Joe and ask that he come to the hospital. The thirty minutes it took him to arrive seemed like hours. Many thoughts raced through my mind, but mostly, all I could think of was holding my poor, precious baby to whom this terrible thing had happened. A very warm, compassionate nurse brought Matt to me. She sat next to the bed, in the small chair provided for visitors, as I held my precious baby. She patted my hand as she told me about all the feelings I might experience— blaming myself, my husband, hating our doctor. She told me she would answer any questions I had, but I couldn't put my thoughts together enough to talk. And then she left, closing the door quietly behind her.

I just held my tiny, sweet boy. I sat on the bed looking at every detail of his little body. And I cried—for him and for me. After

a few minutes, the nurse returned and took Matt back to the nursery. That's about when Joe arrived. We had, and needed, time to ourselves; I was so upset all I could do was cry when he came in the room. Despite what the nurse had said, I started blaming myself, feeling as if I was letting Michael down by not giving him the brother I had promised him. In just two short days, I had fantasized about all the things brothers grow up and do together. Now I felt they would never happen. "How will I explain this to Michael?" I asked Joe. He hugged me and held me tightly. I wanted to be swallowed up in that embrace. I felt like I was falling into a deep, dark hole. Joe's touch brought me comfort and reassurance.

"Tomorrow we will bring a baby brother home for Michael. He's only two. He won't suspect anything is wrong. You have plenty of time to tell him, but it really won't make any difference."

How did Joe know just what I needed to hear? Without saying the words, he assured me that I had not failed as a mother.

Dr. Kenaston told me I could stay an extra day at the hospital if I wanted. But all I could think of was lying in that bed all day with no one I loved around. I felt so very alone, a small speck in an exceptionally large universe. I needed to be near Joe for comfort and strength. So I went home.

There were times, after I was home, that I wondered if I should have stayed where people knew more about this grieving I was doing, who could have helped me through those terrible, rough days. It turns out Joe and Michael were all I needed.

Help Me Teach Him

When Joe, Matt, and I arrived home, our friends Michael and Anna Stafford were waiting there with our big boy, Michael. It was lunchtime, and Anna had made a tuna casserole for us. They were our best friends, and, at that point, were the only ones who knew the secret we had. I couldn't wait to introduce Michael to his baby brother, but he stopped playing only long enough to peek at Matt's little face before he quickly returned to the shiny red Tonka truck he had left on the living room floor.

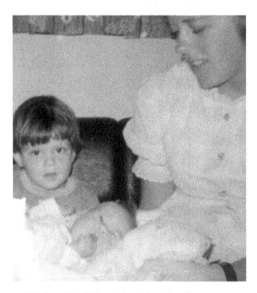

Michael holding Matt for the first time as I prepared to talk to him about Matt. August 1974, Melbourne, Florida

A few days later, I sat Michael down to tell him about the baby. I didn't know what to say, or even how to begin, because I hadn't brought him the baby brother that I thought I would. Knowing I was letting Michael down, sadness filled my heart. He was not getting a buddy to do all the sneaky, silly, wonderful things that brothers do together. I was sure Michael had somehow been cheated.

I gathered him close to me, as I sat on the sofa and placed Matt on a pillow on Michael's lap. Carefully, I chose my words, "Michael, Mommy needs your help." He looked at me; his eyes filled with confusion. I hesitated and took a deep breath before I spoke again.

In the space of that breath I could hear my mother's voice admonishing me to not have a second child. It was Thanksgiving of 1973. I did not yet know that our family was about to grow. We had invited some friends and my mother to join us. Our home was small but we somehow managed to find room for a gathering of friends and family. Food was spread across the dining table, and everyone served themselves buffet-style, and then found a spot to eat, using their laps as tables. After we had stuffed ourselves with turkey, dressing and all the traditional foods, and after some time of holiday conversation, most of the guests departed. My friend, Bobbie, her son, Jeffery, Michael, and I went into the single-car garage that Joe had transformed into a play spot for toys, blocks, and trucks. We had raised the garage door and placed a screened frame in the opening. Often, it was still quite warm in Florida in late November, so having a fresh breeze made it a comfortable place to relax out of the sun.

Mother joined us as we three sat in lawn chairs, engaging in all sorts of women-talk, while the boys played on the carpeted floor. Bobbie mentioned that she and her husband, Hank, were only children. Their plan was for Jeffery also to be an only child. I shared that I had always wanted two children and to have them close together like my sister and I had been.

Mother added to the conversation, "Jadene, if you have another child you will have to share the love that is meant for Michael." Her words pierced my heart—imagine how I felt when I heard them as I was her second child! But I knew it didn't work that way for me. Joe and I had plenty of love to share with any children we would have.

I pushed that memory from my mind. I now had a new baby—a second child—who needed a lot of attention and would need our help for a lifetime. I looked at his little face and then at Michael, who was already getting restless. I continued, "Matt has a boo-boo and it's going to be harder for him to learn all the things you already know. So, I'm going to need you to help him learn. You can teach him how to walk and talk and play."

By now, Michael was squirming, trying to get back to his toys.

I put my arm around him and simply said, "I know you are going to be a wonderful big brother for Matt. Can you help me teach him, Michael?"

He nodded his little head as he slid off the sofa; he needed to get to the blocks scattered about the floor. He was done with our heart-to-heart chat; in his two-year-old eyes, his brother was perfect. After all, there were block towers to build and knock down.

At that time, I didn't realize just how profound that moment was. It was then that my lessons began; I was about to start learning from my best teachers!

My boys showed me it didn't matter what label the doctor gave Matt. Michael helped me see that Matt's tiny fingers and slanted eyes described his brother but didn't define him. Matt's blue eyes danced when he heard our voices—especially Michael's, and that tiny little finger, with the telltale Down syndrome curve, fit perfectly around my own finger. Michael was right, Matt was perfect!

As Matt grew, I imagined new dreams for his life. I was sure that he would be the child with Down syndrome who learned things quicker and better than any of the others.

I Wasn't Doing Enough

When Matt was about twenty months old, Joe and I took the boys from their beds early one morning on a five-hour drive to Miami. Matt had an important appointment at the Mailman Center for Child Development—a children's clinic with pediatric professionals who knew all about babies with Down syndrome.

Matt and I had lost sleep the two previous nights. I had already learned that many babies and toddlers with Down syndrome have a lot of respiratory problems, and Matt was no different. He struggled to breathe as I held him in our tiny bathroom. It was during nights like this that I was more grateful for this little space—just big enough for a tub, the toilet and a small sink and cabinet. With barely enough room to turn around, the bathroom filled quickly with steam from the hot shower. Matt used so much energy trying to fill his little lungs with air, and with each breath a sound like a foghorn shattered the otherwise silent night. After two days and nights of constant attention and broken sleep, Matt's breath finally came easier. I relaxed a little and tried to rest when Matt did—which wasn't easy because Michael needed me, too.

Exhausted, we managed to locate the Mailman Center, and Joe found a place to park. I was worried and excited at the same time. I wasn't sure what the day would bring. All I knew was that Matt was going to be checked by lots of doctors, nurses, and other professionals. The children's center was quite large, and my nervousness grew by the minute as we made our way to the front door and searched to find where we were to go.

One by one, the specialists took him to their private spaces where they tried to get him to do all sorts of tests. Matt's little body was tired from the lost sleep and stressed from the disrupted schedule. He didn't do many of the things they wanted him to do. While Matt was with the professionals, Joe and I answered what seemed like hundreds of questions from other specialists. Late that afternoon, we sat with everyone who had spent those short blocks of time with Matt. I had hoped they would tell me what I could do to help him learn. Instead, I was told that Matt, who was nearly two years old, was functioning like a six-month-old baby. Not one of them factored in the information I had shared about how exhausted my little boy was, having not slept well for days. I felt a pain in my heart, and the knot in my stomach grew larger as I listened, over and over, to those strangers tell me that I wasn't doing enough to stimulate my child.

"I wasn't doing enough?" I had thought. I couldn't imagine what more I could do. I played with Matt; I talked to him whenever I held him, fed him, or changed his diaper. Michael entertained him with their toys. We read books together. I gathered information about Down syndrome from everywhere I could. I was hungry to learn what I could do to help Matt grow. But that was not enough? At least that's what all the professionals believed. On the long walk back to the car, thoughts that my child would be a superstar evaporated and I suddenly felt like a failure as a mom. Had I let Matt down?

Like the words to the old Beatles song say, life goes on. It certainly did for me. Even though I was unhappy for Matt, and felt sorry for myself, I knew that once we got back home, I would need to make meals, do the laundry, give the boys their baths, and play with them. I also knew that I had a husband who adored me and needed his own attention, and I had to find the time and energy for him, as well. Having

those responsibilities helped me to drown out the words of people who didn't really know my child. They certainly didn't see what we were doing at home.

I returned from Miami to my daily routine. But now I was lost. I had no idea how we would get wherever life was taking us. In time, and because my son is a patient teacher, I learned that one diagnosis and one evaluation didn't have to crush my world. And that is not all I have learned.

Learning Matt had Down syndrome had crushed the dreams I had envisioned while I waited for him to join our family. I created new dreams, but dreams can be shattered, even after we make new ones.

Throughout Matt's life I found myself reframing dreams. As Matt has grown to be a middle-aged man, I find my dreams for him now focus more on his health and happiness, rather than his accomplishments. I take comfort in watching him live his everyday life. The dream when he was twenty-two was that he would have his own life, living away from Joe and me. Michael moved out and created a life; Matt deserved to do the same. And he did.

Because he was seen as trouble when he was in school, I dreamed that new people who met him would see the wonderful person I knew. And they did.

Now when I ask what it is about Matt that makes that happen, I hear words like, "sweet," "kind," "loving," and, "funny." Through the years, several staff have insisted that Matt stay on their caseload when they cut back their work schedules. My dreams included a world where Matt was valued by others. And he is.

For over nine years (before COVID made him stop) he was a treasured volunteer at the Bay Pines Veterans Administration Health Care System near his home in St. Petersburg. In many ways, Matt has lived a life that surpassed my dreams.

My life with Matt has shown me that:

- Dreams are not reality, and they can be reframed—many times, if necessary.

- With each new day, I have the chance to start again.

- I could choose to be sad because Matt faced challenges, or I could choose to celebrate him. I choose celebration!

My Gift to You

What are dreams for the future? They can be explained as goals or wishes for what we would like to have happen in our lives. Every one of us will have different goals or dreams based on what we hope to accomplish. When we think about our dreams for the future, our subconscious will work hard to make them happen. But sometimes, we get thrown a curve ball and the specifics of our dream may show up in life differently than we had thought or expected. Rather than being discouraged, we can let the curve balls provide opportunities to change or reframe those dreams, for an outcome that enriches our lives.

Take a few minutes to reflect on some of the dreams that have been important to you.

1. When you were young and thought of your life as an adult, what were your dreams? *In the space below or on a separate piece of paper, write about what you wanted to do as an adult, where you would live, who your family would be.*

_____

_____

_____

2. Was there ever an event in your life that affected the outcome of a dream you had? *Describe the dream you had and the event that disrupted that dream.*

   _____

   _____

   _____

3. What did you do? Did you modify your dream, or let go of it? Did you adjust the dream to meet the new circumstances in your life? *Write about how the event changed that dream.*

   _____

   _____

   _____

A GIFT OF FEELINGS

Dear Matt,

Do you remember when we lived in Germany and there was a carnival in the little towns around us almost every weekend? I cherish memories of your love for the carnival rides, the ones that scare me. You were about ten years old and got so excited when you saw them set up in a field that had been, just days before, empty. We only stopped for you to play when Michael was with us because he would go on those awful rides with you. At the end of every ride you came back to your daddy and me with the biggest grin on your face, your eyes dancing, and your hands signing "play" and "more." There was never a ride that frightened you—not even the roller coasters.

Carnival rides always make me think of the feelings I've had throughout your life. Most have no constant speed, no specific direction, and no predictability. Roller coasters—the worst for me—seem to resemble most closely all the emotions I've had. I could ride to the highest peak with moments of extreme happiness, only to plunge to the lowest valley filled with despair, and then rise once again to a place of joy.

Matt, I am thankful that, because you shared your life with me, I have had many opportunities to experience those feelings and emotions. Sometimes there were sad periods—like when you went away to the residential school in Germany. And there were times that became the best parts of my life, the moments I felt such joy in sharing an accomplishment you made—like touching the heart of a veteran who couldn't be reached.

I've learned that all emotions are important in my life. They have made me softer yet stronger, calm yet excitable, thoughtful yet driven. Your gift of feelings has served me well.

Love,
Momma

A Gift of Feelings

"The emotion that can break your heart
is sometimes the very one that heals it . . ."
Nicholas Sparks, Author,
At First Sight

I began my adult life with a sense of unworthiness. Although I entered my marriage filled with hope and great love, there also was a shadow of doubt that it would last. Those first years of marriage had their challenges, as many do—it's when couples define how life together will be lived.

When the sudden discovery of a forever disability was added to the equation, life looked bleak to me. I feel I must remind you that in the 70s, a baby born with a disability was seen by many doctors as a bad birth. There were long periods of silence when my baby was introduced to family and friends. There were no "welcome baby" gift baskets celebrating the new life that had joined the world. So, there it was—a darkness creeping into my life.

Dark Storm Clouds

Drained of joy, I felt hopelessness begin to take over. Day after day, I walked around our home, going through the routines to keep life moving forward. Three times a day, I stood at the kitchen window, washing dishes from a meal I had just served. The warm, sudsy water would calm me for a moment, and then the dark would fill back in.

I took the boys for walks in our neighborhood every day. With Michael sitting in the back of the double stroller, and Matt in front, we strolled and waved hello at the neighbors. Some were out pruning their palm trees, some were sweeping their sidewalks, and others were just enjoying the warm, sunny Florida day. I became a pro at pasting a smile on my face and making polite social conversation with those neighbors, who didn't have a clue how my heart had broken. Even as Joe tried to help me understand that we wouldn't always have a "less-than" life, I colored my thoughts in black and blue. It seemed the dark storm clouds would always hang over me and I would feel sad forever. While the boys napped, I would dust and quietly clean, some days taking the time to run a cloth quickly over the television that swallowed one end of the living room, or the stereo cabinet, tucked into the only place it would fit, the small dining area where our table and chairs filled the remaining space. There was always something to do to fill my hours as a mother and a wife.

With love and patience, Joe opened the door for me to perceive life differently. Instead of seeing every problem as a mountain,

I started to view our life through the lens Matt had brought to us. My heart is lighter now that I have learned to slow down and to stay out of that hole that darkens my view. And if I find myself in that space, I've learned ways to crawl back out and see the beauty in even the smallest, or most difficult experiences. But it wasn't easy to get there. Sometimes, it still isn't.

Emotions and Thrill Rides

Matt's diagnosis of Down syndrome left me sad and angry. I felt I had been cheated and given a losing hand to play in this game of life. It took me a number of years to see the wonder of all the emotions I experienced. There were many—so numerous that there were times I thought of them as a sack full of wire coat hangers all tangled together. It is tough to pull one, single hanger from the bag without many others coming, too. It had become impossible to know if I was sad, angry, worried, fearful, ashamed, or guilty. Sometimes even the happy emotions were tangled with feelings of guilt.

Years ago, I created a presentation about disability entering our lives. One evening when Matt was about sixteen years old, I stood in front of a group of parents in the fellowship hall of one of our local churches. The room was large—much larger than needed for the small number of moms that sat in metal folding chairs, facing me. Even so, the reception was warm as I shared with them the large brown box with a mailing label addressed to the Ransdells. As I opened that oversized parcel, it was filled with smaller, gift-wrapped boxes. One-by-one, I untied the ribbons and carefully removed the pretty papers. When I found the medium-sized box tied in a multi-colored curly ribbon with lots of long spiraled tails, I unwrapped it and showed that it was filled with feelings. I explained how I was astonished as I learned about all the emotions I faced living with the challenges that Matt's disability brought to us—and how necessary they were to my growth and understanding.

The cliché of an emotional roller coaster is quite appropriate. Roller coasters frighten me. I look at them and immediately get a knot in my stomach. Many are quite high with lots of loops and twists. My fear of heights is just the beginning of my certainty that they are not safe to ride. When we lived in Germany, peer pressure pushed me to ride one with Joe and his friends at the Oktoberfest in Munich. I reminded Joe that I didn't like them and he insisted I would be fine. I was sure I wouldn't be.

My legs trembled as we slowly made our way to the car we were given. Unsteady in high spaces, I was already shakey as I was strapped in and thought about how far above the ground the tracks were. The car jolted as we began to move. We climbed slowly, and followed some gentle curves at the beginning, but I could see what was ahead for us. As we barely moved forward on that steep long, sickening climb to the pinacle of the ride, I knew that the terrifying descent would be filled with left and right curves, and loops that would turn us upside down. It was at that point I was sure I wouldn't make it back to the starting gate without getting sick or passing out. I was frightened and tears flowed.

Looking back on that ride, I recognize the similarity between that roller coaster and the emotions I experienced as I raised Matt. The ride looked and felt unsafe. There were deliberate triggers for fear by making me fall; by turning me upside down; by accelerating rapidly; decelerating suddenly; making me lose my balance; making me dizzy. And then it was over. I was back on the ground and felt safe once again.

The twists and turns, the depths, and heights, can characterize some of the emotions that have accompanied me on this journey. There have been situations that pushed me into emotions that felt unsafe:

And then life brought me back to the safe spaces filled with comforting feelings:

Unpacking Emotions

There's also a cognitive dissonance in thrill rides. You experience the feeling of falling and the illusion of being out of control while knowing in the back of your mind that it is actually regulated and safe—and it won't last forever. That same cognitive dissonance was part of my life raising Matt. It took a few years, but I finally realized that those hard, out of control feelings do get replaced with those that are safe and more comfortable. Let me share some of the feelings I found in that little gift box with the curly ribbons.

When I opened it, I discovered that it was crammed full. Unpacking all the emotions was a challenge. I had learned that the feelings parents encounter are all part of grief, acceptance, and adjustment after they discover their child has a disability. There was a wise psychologist in Illinois, Dr. Ken Moses, who learned from the families he cared for. When he shared his observations, the way we look at parental reactions to their child's disabilities changed. He helped us recognize that a feeling of loss is not unusual when a child is diagnosed with a disability. Grief is part of the reaction to the loss of our dreams, and it is a healthy response. Acknowledging those feelings, and working with them can bring us to the other side—the place where we find happiness, contentment, and joy.

Dr. Moses recognized that the parents he saw in his professional practice poured their deepest grief out to him in therapy sessions. And some of those parents were on the board of the nonprofit for which he worked. Those moms made decisions about the operations of that agency and behaved as rational, "normal," women in their day-to-day lives. They were not dysfunctional, or pathological, at all. Only in therapy did he see the distraught sides of them. Gradually, he came to understand that these moms were grieving. He saw them moving through the stages of grief as if their children had died. But they hadn't died. As he continued to work with the moms he discovered that what they were grieving was the loss of the dreams they had for their children. They were mourning the loss of the child they had imagined as they learned to go on with their lives, loving the

child they now had, letting go of the dreams and creating new dreams for the future.

When I studied Dr. Moses' work, I felt he knew me personally. I already knew that I spent most of my life being a loving mother and wife, a good daughter, sister, and friend, as well as a reliable employee. As a family involvement specialist in our local school district, I worked with families of children enrolled in special education classes. I wrote articles for newsletters, created training workshops for parent groups, and provided individual support to families through phone calls and personal get-togethers for coffee. I used what I learned to help other families recognize the feelings they were experiencing. I helped them to accept those feelings—even the difficult ones like fear and anger. Most importantly, I helped families create new dreams for their children and themselves for a future that was filled with love and hope.

Dr. Moses helped parents understand that their feelings were normal and necessary. And, importantly, *that the emotions had to be shared in order to move on.* Sharing feelings of anger helps us to redefine what is just and fair in our world. Sharing what we feel deeply (and sometimes secretly) helps us form new perceptions of ourselves and our world. Through sharing feelings we can find the strength within us, and the support from others that helps us redefine our dreams. How wonderful it has been to learn this because Matt shared his life with me!

I have kept some of my life moments tucked away on a shelf in my emotional closet. Some have been happy and some of them were difficult. I'm inviting you to peek into my closet for a moment.

- **Guilt and sadness engulfed me when Matt was about a year old.** I had driven our station wagon to a local shopping center. As I took the boys from their carseats and put them in their double stroller, I saw a mom across the parking lot who had two healthy boys about the same age. I was suddenly drowning in sadness and envy. My heart filled with jealousy, certain that she was going to get to live out all the dreams I had that had been crushed by Matt's diagnosis. And then I felt guilty for even thinking those things. I walked slowly into the store. There I purchased what we had come for. With a heavy heart, I reversed our steps back to the car. It took me days to shake the sadness (and guilt) from that short excursion.

- **Every parent who is tired of changing diapers is thrilled when their little one is finally toilet trained. I was no different.** But, do you know anyone who sent out toilet training announcements? I did. I was overjoyed when I could get rid of wet and dirty diapers (cloth ones for too many years to count) because Matt, at nine years old, was wearing big boy underwear. I had begun to think that day would never arrive, but it had and I was proud, happy, and quite giddy. I drew one small card that proclaimed, "We are proud to announce," written in large letters on the front. Opening the little card, it continued, "toilet training success!" I spent hours lettering and coloring the card so that it looked as special as the event I was sharing. I sent it across the ocean from our home in Germany to my dear friend, Anna in Georgia. I knew she would understand and share my joy.

- **There was also a time I felt anger and resentment.** The father of another child with Down syndrome told me that it was obvious why Matt was not speaking, had many difficult behaviors, and was considerably more delayed than other kids his age with Down syndrome. He arrogantly pronounced that I hadn't set expectations high enough for Matt. Well, there was a bucket of feelings dumped on my head! Along with the anger and resentment, I again felt a sense of failure. One more time that I was certain I hadn't been a good-enough mom. The interesting part of this recollection is that the time and location of the conversation have faded from my memory. But the sting of the feelings has not changed.

As Matt grew, the carnival ride of emotions continued to push and pull me. There were lots of ups and downs, twists and turns, and plenty of curves thrown at me. But I learned that those scary times gave me many opportunities to stop, think, reflect, and find a way out. As I worked my way through the daunting days filled with tough feelings, I came to greatly appreciate the sense of comfort and peace I found on the other side.

After years of frustration filled with fear for Matt's future as an adult, the most amazing thing happened. He threw me for a most wonderful loop.

Matt had been working for about eight months as a volunteer at our Bay Pines Veterans Administration Health Care System. I remember vividly the joy I felt the day a social worker told me how much the staff valued him. Tears of happiness filled my eyes when I learned that he had connected with a veteran that the professional staff had been unable to reach. Matt, with his smile and warm heart, got a deeply scarred fellow to smile back and speak to him,

Matt worked as a volunteer at the local VA Health Center for more than nine years. He loved his job and "his soldiers." Bay Pines, Florida

something the clinical staff had unsuccessfully attempted to do for several years. I was beaming and filled with pride for what he had accomplished. The joy I felt was indescribable as his worth was recognized by others. Very few, outside of his family, had valued him in this way before.

It's never too late to explore the feelings wrapped around your heart. Find yourself a friend you trust—it may or may not be your spouse or significant other—and let yourself share. Talk it through without judgment. Your feelings are neither good nor bad but they must be heard and validated.

I've entertained incredibly sad feelings along with delightfully happy ones. By now, I must say that I will be forever grateful that I got to experience every one of them. The negative emotions have been crucial to my growth and have led me to be more open and compassionate. And the enjoyable emotions have provided much sweetness to my life.

Until I understood the process of sorting through and dealing with all those crazy, mixed-up emotions, I was stuck. Once I allowed myself the time to truly feel, to experience the good and the bad, I found my attitude shifted, my heart filled with hope, and life became sweeter. The most wonderful part of allowing myself to experience that gift filled with emotions was a complex understanding that I could:

- Embrace the hard feelings of guilt, anger, sadness, and fear because I knew they would not be forever.

- Cherish the uplifting, positive emotions such as joy, happiness, hope, and contentment that are sweeter following the difficult ones.

- Appreciate the spectrum of emotions and experiences that have given me truly rare and valuable gifts: compassion and empathy.

My Gift to You

Life can be filled with many emotions. Acknowledging our feelings is important to good health. Feelings accompany emotional states that shouldn't be judged as either bad or good—they just are. It is important, though, to recognize how we act on those feelings. Feelings of anger are natural and OK; acting out that anger in a way that hurts yourself or someone else is not. Let's spend a few moments reflecting on emotions or feelings you experience in your life.

There are many times in our lives that we can experience loss. The loss of a dream can bombard us with emotions, some of which we have never before felt. Learning to sort through the highs and lows, the confusion, and the uncertainty, can become one of our greatest gifts.

1. Think back on a time when you faced a loss in your life. It may have been a job, a car, a home, a relationship, or other sort of loss. What are some of the emotions that you experienced at that time? Check all that apply.

   ❑ Denial
   ❑ Anxiety
   ❑ Depression
   ❑ Guilt
   ❑ Anger
   ❑ Fear
   ❑ Other – please list below

2. Do you find one of those feelings seem to be a default feeling for you? In other words, do you frequently find yourself getting angry, or sad, or feeling guilty as your go-to release valve?

   ❑ What do you do that helps you move through those feelings?
   ❑ Do you have someone you can share your feelings with – even those that trouble you? If not, can you write down how you feel as a way to let it go?
   ❑ Feelings of happiness and joy are also part of our lives, not just those feelings that are labeled as negative. How do you acknowledge and celebrate the good times in your life?

A GIFT OF STRENGTH

Dear Matt,

I can honestly say that my life is rich because more than forty-eight years ago, you chose me to be your mom.

I am thankful that you have given me the gift of strength, one of the most empowering presents I have received from you.

In strength, I acquired the ability to hold on when life got hard—almost unbearable. In strength, I found a voice to speak up and speak out when you and others could not. In strength, I deepened my soul's connection to God and the Divine.

The gift of strength is one that I keep returning to, and I know now that it was one that I desperately needed. Although pain was a part of this gift, I've learned that finding my strength helps me live my life with meaning. I've also learned that there will be times my strength is sapped, but if I hold on I can find it within me once again. Spending time with you is one of the best ways I know to rebuild my strength.

Because you chose me to be your mom, Matt, I have been given many opportunities to grow stronger personally, professionally, and spiritually. Thank you, my wonderful son, for this gift that has changed both our lives.

Love,
Momma

A Gift of Strength

*"Difficulties are meant to rouse, not discourage.
The human spirit is to grow strong by conflict."*
William Ellery Channing,
Unitarian Preacher

Personal Strength

I Wasn't Good Enough

Before Matt joined me in our life, I was timid. I lacked self-confidence and self-worth. My dad was quiet and rarely showed any warm feelings toward my sister and me. Mother, on the other hand, remained silent if we did something well, and was quick to criticize the smallest thing—from how my hair looked and how my makeup was applied, to my weight (I was never extremely overweight, but always bigger than my sister), to the sound of my voice when I spoke or (heaven forbid) sang around the house. I seemed to easily get in trouble with Mother, so I chose to not go to parties with high school friends just to avoid her scorn later. As a result of feeling like I would never make her happy, I always wanted to please people—even if it meant doing something I really didn't want to do.

If bad things happened to me, I figured it was because I wasn't good enough to have it any better. It seemed as if everything in my life turned to trouble. Maybe that's why I never questioned the doctor's diagnosis—after all, what did I deserve? I already had one perfectly healthy child. Did I really deserve two of them?

When Matt joined me in our life, my strength training began.

The Test is Positive

One warm, sunny Saturday in September, I found myself alone with the boys. Caring for a newborn with a disability and a rambunctious two-and-a-half-year-old took a great deal of energy and logistical coordination. However, I was finally getting the hang of it. I was beginning to function relatively well and was comfortable that I could get through a day without Joe to help occupy Michael's time.

On that Saturday, Joe was working with his father, scraping barnacles off the bottom of their cabin cruiser that was in dry-dock at a marina near his father's home. It was not a job Joe enjoyed, but it did give him time to be with his dad. When the pediatrician, Dr. Kenaston, called late in the morning, I had already fed Michael breakfast, given Matt a bottle, and had put him down for his first nap of the day. I had also finished a couple of loads of laundry while Michael played in his garage playroom.

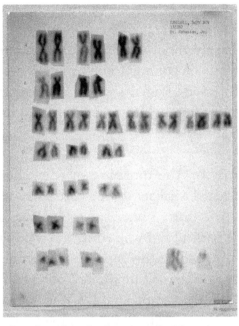

With no emotion in his voice, the doctor said, "I've got the results we've been waiting for. The test is positive; it definitely shows forty-seven chromosomes. When you bring Matt in for his next appointment, I'd like for you to bring your husband, too." He shared no warmth, no compassion; perhaps I should have realized then what was ahead for us.

Results of study showing Matt has three copies of the 21st chromosome.

I could say nothing but agree that we would both be at the next appointment before the tears started to flow. I had known in my heart that the test would confirm the diagnosis, but I didn't expect to hear about it over the phone, and I certainly didn't think I would be alone in the house when I got the results. As soon as the call ended, I gripped the receiver of that yellow wall phone, and dialed my friend Bobbie's number with shaking hands.

"Dr. Kenaston just called," I told her when she answered. "The test is positive."

We chatted briefly and then I waited for Joe to return home. I tried to busy myself with housework and playing with the boys, but I kept hearing Dr. Kenaston's voice in my head. "The test is positive."

That afternoon seemed to drag on forever. It felt like a lifetime before Joe got home and I was able to share the news. He rarely expressed his emotions, so when he heard, he did not react but hugged me tightly as he reassured me that everything would be all right.

Early on the morning of the scheduled appointment, we dropped Michael at Joe's parents' home and then drove silently for the thirty minutes it took to get to Dr. Kenaston's office. We parked and walked to the waiting room. We were feeling hopeful about this appointment because we had been incredibly happy with the care the doctor had provided for Michael. (I felt a special attachment to Dr. Kenaston as his father had been the pediatrician who cured swimmer's ear for Jaren and me when we visited our grandparents every summer.) We knew Dr. Kenaston as a man who cared about his little patients, and as a doctor who had a sense of humor. I still have the prescription for vitamins written for "Fang Ransdell," aka Michael, whose first teeth were his upper canines and not those adorable center-front ones.

As we sat, I glanced around the empty waiting room. I knew this place well and had spent many hours there as a child and with Michael. That day I felt like I had never been there before. There were wood and leather chairs with arms, placed along the walls around the perimeter of the room. In one corner were shelves of books and toys, and there was a child-sized table and chairs for the little ones to sit at while they waited to be seen. Sitting in that room with Joe and my baby, I thought back on the night Dr. Kenaston had told me of his suspicion. Now we had confirmation. I felt anxious but was certain the doctor was going to tell us how to help Matt. The nurse motioned for us to follow her and led us into the exam room. She instructed me to remove Matt's clothes and booties, except for his diaper. In a few minutes, Dr. Kenaston joined us and went through the motions of a typical well-baby check. He listened to Matt's heart. He measured the circumference of his head and the length of his body. He recorded his weight, checked his reflexes. He then asked me about Matt's eating and sleeping schedule. Dr. Kenaston said nothing about Mongolism. I thought that was strange.

When the doctor finished the checkup, he said, "Go ahead and dress Matt and then meet me in my office." As he had done in the hospital on the night he shattered my dreams, he left us alone with our thoughts. As I quickly dressed my baby, Joe and I didn't speak. I held Matt as Joe gathered the diaper bag and baby carrier, and we left the exam room.

In a few minutes Dr. Kenaston entered his office, walked to his desk, and sat down. His expression was serious. We were sitting across from him, facing the window looking out toward the street and could get just a glimpse of the Indian River beyond the houses.

This is what he said in the brutal language of the time:

"As I told you on the phone, Mrs. Ransdell, the test we did shows Matt has forty-seven chromosomes instead of the normal forty-six. There is an extra copy of the 21st chromosome and this is definitive of Mongolism. You know, children like Matt can't learn very much. I believe you have seen the home across the street for the retarded adult men. There are no Mongoloid men over there because they just can't function well enough, even with help from others. He will never learn to feed himself; he will never be toilet trained. Children like him can cause many problems for their families. He will cause your other son to have emotional problems and the two of you to end up divorced. Children like him are a burden on families. There is a solution to this problem, however. You can place him in Sunland, the state institution in Orlando."

Sunland Orlando where Dr. Kenaston wanted me to take Matt, walk away and then just forget about him.

My heart pounded, and I clutched Matt more tightly. At that moment, I couldn't imagine Matt as an adult. My breath became shallow and the sounds around me began to fade away. I fought tears. I was not prepared for what I was hearing.

He continued, expressionless and without emotion:

"Sunland can provide the care he needs, but it takes a long time to complete all the arrangements. I have already spoken with the social worker over there and have begun some of this process for you." As he pointed to a small stack of papers on the corner of his desk he continued, "All you have to do is sign these forms and we can get this started."

As my mind reeled, I started to feel outrage.

He had already started the process? He wasn't giving us a say in what happens to our baby? I looked at Joe who was staring at the floor, the muscles in his face tight. And I could hear Dr. Kenaston was still talking about sending our baby away forever.

As if everything he said hadn't already crushed my heart, I felt my breath catch in my throat at his final directive:

"Don't take too long making this decision. Babies like Matt are just like puppies, and the longer you have him around, the more attached you will become to him."

Thoughts were swirling through my mind. I was shocked, scared, and confused.

What did he just say?

Did he just compare my precious baby to a puppy?

First, he said Matt is a problem; now he has called him a puppy?

Why would he do that?

Doesn't he understand that Joe and I love this little boy?

He isn't a problem, and he certainly isn't a puppy.

My mind was racing and all I wanted to do was leave. I was shocked. Expecting to get guidance on how to provide the best for my baby, this man was suggesting I abandon my infant. Joe and I looked at each other with stunned expressions. Tears filled our eyes. I could hardly speak, but managed, "We'll think about this; but I don't want to sign anything today."

As quickly as we could, we got out of the office into the safety of our car, and started our journey back to Michael, and Joe's parents.

We drove in silence, filled with hurt,

    filled with confusion,

        filled with hopelessness,

           and helplessness.

I used Matt's gift of strength to hold on tight. The world had turned upside down, and I was sure I was going to fall off. How could anyone suggest that a mother give her baby to someone else to raise! When I looked at his sweet face, I would cry and ask God, "Why have you done this to my sweet, innocent baby?"

Wrapped in a Hug

It took me several months to process what we had been told, and to give Dr. Kenaston my answer. I had been taught to follow a doctor's order, but this didn't feel right. So, to think and sort through my feelings, I flew to Illinois with my boys to visit my Uncle Russel and my Aunt Virginia, my mom's sister.

Aunt Virginia was four years older than my mother and different from her in many ways. They were both medium height and slender build with dark hair and a brunette complexion. That's where any similarity ended. Where mom was moody, Aunt Virginia was happy; I don't remember ever seeing a frown on her face. My mother had a flair for drama, especially when she was upset with someone. Aunt Virginia just went on about her day when people annoyed her; I don't recall her ever speaking poorly about anyone—well, perhaps her stepmother, who none of us liked. And where my mother spent most of her day on the sofa, smoking, drinking coffee, and reading romance novels, Aunt Virginia rarely sat still. She and my Uncle Russel lived on a large farm in west-central Illinois, near Macomb. There were huge shade trees in the yard and a big U-shaped gravel driveway that divided the space between the house and the barns. Beyond the house and barns were acres and acres of fields where corn and soybeans grew every year. In the field just west of the house was a small herd of cows, and often there were a few pigs being fattened in the barn lot north of the driveway. So there was always a lot to do—chickens to feed and eggs to gather. There was a garden to tend and vegetables to be canned. And then there were three large meals every day, laundry, and Sunday school lessons to plan. If Aunt Virginia was found sitting, she would be crocheting, knitting, doing hand embroidery, or playing a church hymn on the piano.

Uncle Russel was a quiet man. He was tall and thin with no hair on the top of his head. He could nearly always be seen in the uniform of a farmer—bibbed overalls, and a cotton shirt with the sleeves rolled up to his elbows. His well-worn hat covered that bald spot whenever he was outside. He was kind, gentle, and soft spoken, yet as kids, my cousins and I obeyed when he gave us directions or told us to be quiet. He was out of the house early every morning (there were no days off for farmers) to get work done before the heat of the day, and he often returned to the barn for another hour after supper was finished. Every weekday at noon, he would sit in his recliner with the local television news station giving the stock market prices—not the prices of major businesses but the farmer's world prices—the latest on grains and livestock. His life, and that of his family, depended on him keeping track of those numbers. I knew that half-hour of the day was to be spent whispering or better yet not talking at all, so that Uncle Russel knew whether it was time to hold or sell. In the evening, especially on hot summer nights, he would fix all of us a dish of vanilla ice cream smothered in Hershey chocolate syrup. To this day, whenever I see that familiar bottle, I recall sweet memories of my Uncle Russel.

I adored my aunt and uncle, who had come to think of me as the daughter they never had. The summer between my freshman and sophomore years in college, Aunt Virginia had a complete hysterectomy, and I lived with them during her six-week recovery. This was no vacation on the farm. With Aunt Virginia in bed, her chores became my chores. I was up before daylight cooking a full breakfast for Uncle Russel and my two younger cousins, Gene and John. The aroma of coffee percolating in the pot on the stove and bread, toasted under the broiler in the oven (and turned at just the right time to get both sides equally brown) were the smells I knew would get the guys to the table before sunrise each morning. Fresh eggs and bacon (from one of the pigs that had been out by the barn not long before) were staples of mornings on the farm. About 11:30, the men made their way back to the house where they would devour pork chops, potatoes, and green beans (or something similar) as they talked about the work they were doing in the fields, or which cow needed some care.

I savored those minutes of togetherness, as each bite they took filled me with a connection to family that I hadn't experienced in my own. Although my days centered on the men's schedule, and I fell into bed exhausted every night, I still found moments to stop and visit with Aunt Virginia. Even confined to her bed or the sofa, she still did her beautiful needlework and shared stories of her life with my mother when they were young girls.

The summer of 1967 was monumental in my life. It was during that time that I unknowingly laid a foundation for building strength as I learned to develop a strong work ethic. And that's not all. It was the first time in my life that I felt a sense of worth; I was needed and appreciated—and loved. It was one of the sweetest periods of my college years.

So, when I wanted space and time to consider what Dr. Kenaston had said, the only place I thought I could do that was on the farm. It was there where I felt safe and knew that I could have the time I desperately needed to put our world right-side up. Uncle Russel was happy to have me with them, and Aunt Virginia let me rest as she delighted in caring for Matt and Michael. We had been there only a day when she expressed concern because Matt would cry and draw his little knees up under his belly after he ate. I was in awe when she called her country doctor who knew just what to do with only a description of Matt's symptoms. Old Doc Mueller had cared for Aunt Virginia, Uncle Russel, and my cousins for many years and, over the phone, he prescribed medicine that he believed would help. In addition to giving Matt the drops, Aunt Virginia would rub his back, gently in tiny circles, until he fell asleep. I was awash in the love and support she gave me; never once did she lecture or try to influence the decision I had to make.

This time, I was the one being cared for completely. Looking back now, those six weeks on the farm in the fall of 1974 were one of the biggest expressions of love that I have ever received. That visit for me was like being wrapped in a hug.

A Life of Love and Hope

Aunt Virginia had made an appointment for me to visit an early intervention program about an hour from the farm. One morning, with a heavy snowstorm forecast, we headed out (I felt loved and supported because Uncle Russel was willing to take time away from his chores and to venture out even though it would probably start snowing before we would get back to the farm). Uncle Russel drove their new white four-door Impala Chevrolet, with Aunt Virginia in the front seat, while Matt and I sat in the back—we had left Michael with my cousin Gene and his wife, Martha. I was so excited because early intervention programs were just beginning in certain parts of the country. I was learning that little babies like mine were going to school.

We first met with the director of the infant program. She then led us into a large room that was filled with moms and little ones with Down syndrome. The room was painted in soft colors with splashes of vibrant primary colors all around. The floors were covered in large, soft area rugs or thick vinyl mats. The mothers and babies were sitting in rocking chairs or upholstered chairs with arms stuffed just enough to be comforting. Some of the little ones were on the floor, and they were learning to roll over, sit up, crawl, or walk. I got to see lots of tiny humans at play, but they were really working hard. Some of the mommies were signing words, and their babies were signing back!

My heart filled with joy and excitement. I saw, with my own eyes, little ones with Down syndrome doing everything that pediatrician had told me Matt would never do. It was at that very moment that I knew I could give him a life filled with love and hope.

Battles with the Public Schools

Matt was born just one year before Public Law 94-142 was passed. That legislation guaranteed a free and appropriate public education to every child with a disability. The law was long and quite complex. I

PL 94-142, the Education of All Handicapped Children Act was enacted in 1975. It has since been replaced with the Individuals with Disabilities Education Improvement Act or IDEA.

remember the first time I read it, I was overwhelmed, and was certain that I would never understand it.

However, I did learn that law. And I was grateful that when Matt started school, those protections were there for him. When Joe went back in the Army after he graduated from college, we moved to Fort Benning, Georgia. It was there that I met several parents of children with intellectual disabilities. Their children were older than Matt and they had been following the legislation for some time. I listened intently as they talked about the different sections of the law and what it all meant. Those wonderful women became mentors to me as I was learning to parent a child with a disability. I used what I learned from those moms many times in Matt's life.

My knowledge of the law gave me the strength to speak up for Matt. I used the law to get Matt enrolled in a kindergarten class. I used the law to get appropriate services for him while we were in Germany, and I used it again when we returned home to the States.

Matt in the fall of 1982; he was having more trouble connecting to us and others. Vogelweh, Germany

When Matt was seven years old, Joe got military orders to Germany. By then Matt had been in three different public-school programs and I had learned the ropes for writing his Individual Education Plan (IEP), one of the key parts of PL 94-142. During those years, Matt struggled to find his place in our world. As Joe and I attempted to help him, the military school system made a referral for behavior management services which were provided only to students who had a label of Severely Emotionally Disturbed. I was assured that the emotionally disturbed label would not follow Matt but be used only within the military school programs.

When we came home from Germany, the battles with the public schools continued. That emotionally disturbed label sparked a prolonged fight when we first returned to the States. When the new school district saw Matt's IEP with an "emotionally disturbed" classification, administrators ignored Matt's needs related to his intellectual disability. Matt was placed in a center-based school filled with students who had significant mental health problems. The students were twice his size, were street-smart, threw desks, and were aggressive to the teachers. I was afraid for him every day and immediately began fighting the placement decision. Under federal law, the district had nearly six weeks to get Matt into an appropriate program. And they seemed prepared to use every one of those days. I made phone calls, I met with the principals of the school Matt had been assigned to, and the school where he should have been enrolled. Both principals agreed that his placement had been inappropriate, yet they could do nothing to move the process more quickly.

Weeks passed and on the Friday morning of the fourth week I had had enough. Matt's needs were not being met and his vulnerability helped me muster the strength to act. Although I was scared about what might happen, I knew it was time to do something. With my stomach churning, my fingers shook as I tapped the buttons on my touchtone phone to contact the district administration office. "Good morning, this is Mrs. Ransdell," I began. "I want you to know that I will enact due process and call my attorney if Matt's placement is not changed by the end of the day," I informed the director of exceptional education programs.

Early that afternoon, I got the call I had been waiting for. Matt would start at the center-based school for students with intellectual disabilities the following Monday and the emotionally disturbed label would be removed from his records.

There were just a few months left of the school year by this time. Matt settled in and adjusted well. The following year was not so good.

I Will Always Fight for You

The teacher Matt was assigned to had previously taught several of the students in her class at a local nonprofit community agency preschool for children with disabilities. When Matt joined her class halfway through the second semester, she had already established a routine and developed a close bond with the children and their parents. To her, Matt was an intruder.

I spent some time with her to share what Matt liked and the sort of things that bothered him. Even with that information, she deliberately put him in situations that caused problems for him. Within a few weeks, the behaviors that Matt exhibited in the classroom led the school staff to recommend we seek the services of a child psychiatrist.

I was always a bit tense during the appointments with this doctor because there were often long waits once we got to his office. At that time, Matt didn't do well with waiting; the longer it took, the louder Matt got. He was twelve years old, nearly as tall as me, and quite strong when he was upset. Sometimes he got agitated while we waited, and I would have to hold him on my lap with my arms wrapped tightly around him. When the doctor finally entered the room, he usually walked in and stayed close to the wall on the opposite side of the office—it seemed as if he was uncomfortable with Matt, which I found strange since he was a child psychiatrist.

This doctor started Matt on Haldol, a very powerful mental health drug. We had agreed that he could speak with Matt's teacher prior to our appointments to get an idea of how he was doing both at home and at school. Every time we saw him, he said that the teacher had claimed Matt was more disruptive than previously reported, and that he bit and pinched other kids. I was surprised by these statements because we were not seeing a rise in difficult behaviors at home, nor had we been informed of these incidents. Still, because of her comments, Matt's medication was increased at every appointment. With every dosage adjustment I noticed changes in Matt that were of growing concern. He was more lethargic, less interactive, and sometimes had unexplained periods of upset where he would be loud, or cry for no apparent reason.

One afternoon in the middle of October, I got a call from Wrex Diem, the school principal. He was a jovial fellow, short, round, and balding. In the few short months that I had known him, I was aware that his students were particularly important to him. The moment I answered the phone, he began, "I thought you should know that there is going to be a parent meeting tomorrow night here at the school. I only learned of it earlier today. Matt's teacher has organized it to talk about how she and the other parents can get Matt out of her classroom. I believe you and Joe might want to attend. I have already asked Mr. Kriever, the area superintendent, and Mrs. Mozelle, the director of the mentally handicapped programs, to attend, as well."

When I heard his words, I was furious that private information about Matt had been shared with other parents. Of course, Joe and I went to the meeting. We arrived about five minutes before the 7 p.m. start time. Turning off the main road, we drove another quarter mile to the parking lot. The self-contained, segregated school campus was very pretty, filled with lush, tropical plantings and canopied by majestic oak trees dripping with Spanish moss. I sometimes wondered if the school was built to be invisible to the Clearwater traffic to hide Matt and his school friends—all of whom had either an intellectual disability or were Autistic.

As Joe parked the car, my hands became sweaty, and I could feel the anxiety build in my stomach and gut. I took many deep breaths as we walked slowly to the door and went inside.

Most of the others were already present and sitting in the hallway in an oval of cold, taupe-colored metal folding chairs, outside the main office. Mrs. Cauffman, the vice principal, was just coming from her office as Joe and I found two seats together. Mrs. Mozelle, a petite, and attractive middle-aged woman, sat between Superintendent Kriever and Principal Diem. They smiled warmly at Joe and me as we sat opposite them. There were some empty seats to my right, and more empty seats next to Joe. At the far-left end of the oval, the other parents and Matt's teacher sat together. By the looks on their faces when we sat down, it was obvious they hadn't expected us to be there.

I was so scared and nervous. I wasn't sure how I was going to get through the meeting without crying. I don't remember a lot of the details of that night, but I know I kept my composure. I mostly listened, but when it was necessary, I spoke for Matt.

Lots of chatter, complaining, and negative comments filled the air. Parents described details of several incidents that I knew nothing about. I wondered how they knew.

"Matt doesn't belong in this classroom," one parent practically shouted. "He should be with the Autistic kids." At that time, Matt did not have an official Autism diagnosis.

I could hardly believe my ears when I heard another parent demand to know, "Isn't Matt on medication for his behaviors?"

I could stay quiet no longer as betrayal and rage grew simultaneously inside me. I thought of Matt. I pictured what it must have been like for him every day he came to school. My heart ached. I glared at the other parents and then locked my eyes on the teacher. With a voice that seemed to come from outside of me, I spoke directly to the teacher, "You have revealed confidential information about Matt."

Suddenly, a sense of calm washed over me, even as my face expressed the anger inside me. "It is not your place to tell others anything about Matt unless I have given you permission. Because I'm also a Florida certified teacher, I know that you have disregarded the very precepts we are bound to uphold. You have not only violated Matt's privacy, but you have stripped him of his dignity and disparaged him to others. I have every reason and every right to seek a solution to this with the administration, and legally, if needed. I hope you understand that these are grounds for which you could lose your teaching certificate."

I had said enough. I stopped talking and the room fell silent. I glanced around to see the eyes of those parents and the teacher cast down toward their laps. Stunned expressions were on many of their faces.

Mr. Kriever, the Area Superintendent, was the first to break the silence.

"Matt is in the most appropriate placement and there will be no change in his classroom. I am instructing Mrs. Mozelle to make observations and to assist the teacher to structure the classroom and the schedule to better meet the educational needs of the students, especially Matt. I expect the teacher to provide Mrs. Mozelle with detailed lesson plans for the remainder of the school year."

The meeting came to an end quickly after that. As Joe and I returned home, we talked about what had happened. The realization of what Matt's teacher had done was sinking in, and I told Joe that I was sad for Matt. He couldn't communicate in a way that people understood; he was frustrated and acted out because of it. Tears streamed down my face as I thought of Matt being treated differently than his classmates.

Matt had given me the strength I needed to stand up and speak out for him. He was asleep when we got home, but I opened the door to his bedroom and tiptoed to his bed. I placed the softest kiss on his forehead, as I silently promised, "I will always fight for you."

The next morning I got a call from Mr. Diem.

"Jadene, I just spoke with Mr. Kriever, and I wanted to let you know how moved he was with the way you and Joe handled last night's meeting. He said you have every right to sue the teacher and the school district and is impressed that you remained calm and thoughtful even as terrible things were said about Matt. He wants you to know that the teacher will be watched closely and will most likely be reassigned at the end of the school year."

The remainder of that school year was tense. After several classroom visits, the administrators found that Matt's schedule was not conducive to learning and that the teacher was, indeed, setting Matt up for problems by the way she planned her activities. At that time, Matt's attention span was short, and he didn't sit still to watch TV. Yet every morning she had circle time, and during that period she didn't talk to or interact with her students, instead she turned on the local PBS channel for thirty minutes or more of *Sesame Street*.

Kids in wheelchairs used to upset Matt. Mrs. Mozelle, in her classroom observations, found that even though the teacher knew this, and even though the classroom was quite large, she still sat him extremely close to students who used wheelchairs. The situation in the classroom was periodically monitored by the school and district administrators for the remainder of the school year. The next year she was transferred to another school.

And Relentlessly, I Remind Them

Matt's gift of strength has bolstered me many times throughout his life. There are sometimes disagreements with some of Matt's doctors. And there are battles with the state agency who provides funding for his services. I have had to be strong when I fought to let him live in the home he has chosen. I had to fight to ensure he could volunteer with the veterans with whom he loved working. It hasn't been easy, but Matt is worth every ounce of strength it takes to help him create the life he has a right to live.

For more than twenty years, Matt has lived in a home of his choosing with staff support that is paid for through the Developmental Disabilities Home and Community-Based Services (DDHCBS) Waiver. Florida residents who have a developmental disability and have been approved by the state can receive a variety of services that help them to live as independently as possible in their community.

The state officials who make the rules about those services have, on more than one occasion, claimed that Matt doesn't have enough skills to live in his own home and have tried to push me to move him to a group home.

Matt moved out of our home in 1997 and has lived in his own place since then. He enjoys his adult life and still loves to come visit us.

Many times, I have had to remind them of their claim to a person-centered focus on service delivery. I remind them that Matt does have a right to live in a home of his choosing with the supports that are necessary to keep him safe and healthy. I remind them that he has always done better when he is in a family-like setting, and that he has a right to have an adult life just as his brother does. He has that now, with a housemate, Chris, who has become a good friend. The two of them are like brothers—getting on each other's nerves and missing each other when they are separated.

Because there is a very long waiting list, the state of Florida often conducts an exercise to reduce the budgeted funds available to recipients for their needed services. Those drills sometimes become big battles. These conflicts aren't fought with fists or guns but with lots and lots of paper. We must send the state employees information about Matt—justification for why he needs the supports he does. It makes my head spin and my eyes cross. I often get frustrated and find it silly, because no matter what they may think, Matt will always have Down syndrome. He will never have less need for supports, as he will not suddenly wake up one morning and be a different person (and who would ever want that to happen?). And so, relentlessly, I remind them of the worth Matt has as a human being and how brightly his star shines. Some of the strength that Matt has given me has led me to be persistent and to keep advocating, even when I get worn down and worn out.

Professional Strength

"Just a Parent"

My career path has been directly influenced by sharing my life with this man who was given an extra copy of that tiny chromosome. Looking back, I love the way it has unfolded. As a young girl, I loved being with the little ones in our neighborhood. The moms I gave respite to all declared I would make a wonderful teacher—and so I went off to learn how to educate kindergarteners. I mean, isn't that everyone's favorite teacher?

My path to becoming a teacher got interrupted with a move from Iowa to Florida, my marriage, and our two babies. When Michael was a toddler, his energy level led me to believe I could never handle a classroom filled with children with his exuberance. I changed my mind about becoming a teacher.

However, teaching came back on my radar with Matt's birth. I quickly came to realize that observations I shared with professionals about my son were dismissed because I was "just a parent." Those dismissals only strengthened my resolve to be a strong advocate for my boy.

The move to Fort Benning, Georgia, when Matt was not quite three, ultimately led me to enroll in Columbus College with the encouragement of one of the mothers I had met. In sixteen months, I completed my final two years of college, humbled and surprised when I was presented the Graduate of the Year Award in the Special Education program. It was during my classes that I came to realize that sharing my experiences with Matt was helpful to the classmates in my education courses. I still did not want to be a classroom teacher and had only pursued a bachelor's degree in education as a way to open doors, open eyes, and ears, and to put me in a position to support families like ours.

I took extra classes every quarter so I could graduate by the time Joe's Army assignment ended. Being a student, a wife, and the mother of two young boys wasn't easy. I was fortunate that the living quarters we had been assigned were small and easy to clean, saving me time for studying. Joe pitched in by caring for the boys while I was in class and keeping them occupied while I studied. He sometimes made supper and did the dishes, gave the boys their baths, and would put them to bed whenever I had an evening class that ran later than their bedtime. It took teamwork for me to complete my education, and I will never forget what Joe did to help me.

That degree opened many doors, and the life experiences shared with Matt gave me a perspective that has been valuable in every job I have had. Although I never planned to be a classroom teacher, I have taught in several schools and the same state institution where the pediatrician had suggested we send Matt. Classroom teaching was such a small part of my career; family support and advocacy was my passion.

I grew stronger and more effective as a family advocate as a result of providing the support that Matt needed. I was shy and timid when Matt was born. It didn't take long for me to realize that if I didn't speak up on his behalf, Matt would be denied many of the services he needed. Strength grew in me from the experiences we encountered. My advocacy voice, as a parent first, and then as a professional, has changed from the mew of a weak, little kitten to the roar of a strong, powerful lioness!

"You are Strong"

Within a year of our relocation to Germany with the US Army, Matt started having a hard time in school. He still had very limited verbal communication, and at that time, I didn't know why he seemed to always be upset and found it challenging to be in large groups. Life got awfully hard for him. His smiles and giggles disappeared.

Michael and Matt attended an elementary school that was run by the Department of Defense Dependent Schools (DoDDS). It was the first time both boys attended the same school, and I was loving that. Although the first year went relatively smoothly, Matt showed an increase in troubling behaviors in his second and third years. Two teachers taught his class the first and second years. In the third year, the teacher Matt worked better with had moved to the high school with the older students. That's when Matt became less cooperative, and we got many notes home about his behaviors. One afternoon, I got a call from the principal who told me that as Matt walked down the hallway to his classroom, he ran away from the group, yanked student artwork off the wall, and ripped it beyond repair. That was just one of many troubling incidents at school—incidents that left us wondering what was happening to him. My heart ached hearing this news.

The Heim mit Sonderschule is where Matt lived and went to school
the last eleven months we were in Germany. Herxheim, Germany

Ultimately, the administrators decided they would no longer
serve Matt in their school. We had many meetings with the
teacher, school administrators, medical personnel, and DoDDS
regional staff to discuss what we could do. Eventually, Matt was
sent to a German residential school in a town about forty-five
minutes from our home, where his new principal had a limited
use of the English language and where the house parents spoke
no English.

From the moment that we were informed Matt could not attend
the neighborhood school, I struggled with my thoughts. I was
heartsick as I came to realize that he would soon leave us. And
then the day arrived when I had to walk away from him.

Our friends, Mary Vivian (who we all called Marv) and Doug
Mantooth, drove us to Herxheim early one morning in February
1985. Doug was one of Matt's teachers when we first transferred

to Germany not quite three and a half years before. We had become good friends as we tried to unravel Matt's mysteries. Doug and Marv anticipated that this day would be difficult and just wanted to help us get through it. The morning sky mirrored my mood: somber and overcast with dampness that dripped on my face. I don't remember much of the trip, except for the intense ache in my heart as I hugged and kissed my little boy goodbye. A painful day for Joe and me, as we left our eleven-year-old son in the care of strangers in a country where we didn't speak the language.

Late that afternoon, we arrived back home. The four of us, cold from the damp winter weather and fatigued from an exceptionally long day, walked slowly and silently up the three flights of stairs to the apartment to which I didn't want to return. Michael was spending the night with one of his friends, so our quarters were empty when we arrived home. Quiet by nature, Joe spoke little; head down and shoulders slumped, he unlocked the door to our quarters, walked straight into the living room, turned on the television and tuned out for the rest of the evening. Marv settled in with Joe to watch, in silence, whatever was on the small screen.

Exhausted from saying goodbye to my little boy, I had nothing left to give and only wanted to drown the overwhelming sadness I was feeling. I took one of my delicately etched French wine glasses from the kitchen cupboard, along with a bottle of my favorite German white wine and sat them on the table. Opening the refrigerator, I found cold beers for the others.

Doug asked if I wanted to stay in the kitchen and chat, rather than watch whatever program was on the television. I recall how happy I usually was in my kitchen, but not on that day. Even the brightly colored German pottery that decorated the walls and shelves did nothing to brighten my mood. I was numb.

As he slid into the bench at the back of the table, I took a seat on one of the small wooden chairs where Michael and Matt usually sat. Doug took a long sip of beer and said, "Jadene, I know you're in pain and are deep in thought. Tell me what's on your mind."

I started to cry. Then I took a deep breath and sobbed, "Why would anybody listen to anything I have to say about kids with disabilities? Obviously, I don't know what to do and I'm just a phony! I'm not even a good enough mother to keep her little boy with his family. I have no business thinking I can help others when I can't even help my own child."

Doug reached across the table and patted my hand.

"You know, we're really good friends, Jadene, and I've always been honest with you. What you just said is just not true. You are a wonderful mother to both of your boys, and you have so much to offer other parents. So many families who have kids with severe disabilities are being stationed here; think of how many moms you have spoken with in the past few months. You've told me they desperately needed to know that someone really understood their personal pain. I'm thinking about the Air Force pilots' wives who have not slept in days as they care for their children who aren't sleeping due to their disabilities. You've told me those moms are alone while their husbands are away for weeks at a time.

"So, I want you to look at this separation from Matt, not as a failure, but as an opportunity to learn. Take what you discover and use it to support all these families that the military is bringing to Germany—families who don't have support. They need you. Tonight, you can cry. Tomorrow, you're going back to your office at the Army Community Services center, and you will be there to answer the phone when another mom calls you. You may not feel it today, but I'm telling you, you are strong. You can do this. I know you can."

While I didn't believe Doug at that moment, his faith in me gave me the courage to continue my work as an advocate. I returned to my office the next morning, shaken but filled with resolve to help families coming along behind me. With each passing day, I felt stronger, knowing that Matt was finally getting the support he needed and knowing that I could help families who felt isolated.

Many times, through the decades since that day of heartbreak, I have heard Doug's voice.

"You are strong. You can do this."

Those words have echoed in my mind and have encouraged me to keep sharing my knowledge and my experiences with other families. Even today, more than forty years later, I hear Doug gently nudging me to not give up. For that I am forever grateful.

Offering Guidance, Encouragement, and Hope

The strengths I have gained, as I learned to be a strong advocate for Matt and others, steered me professionally as well as personally. I live in gratitude that Matt's need for my support instilled a strength in me to confidently take on responsibilities that just a few short years before I would have never considered. In addition to the leadership role I enjoyed in the American military community while we lived in Germany, I was the first executive director of the Family Network on Disabilities of Florida, a state-wide nonprofit focused on families of young children and students with disabilities. The organization was the home of the federally funded Parent Training and Information Center in Florida as well as the headquarters for Parent-to-Parent support in the state.

As a private consultant, I worked with the Florida Department of Education to instruct parents and teachers in collaboration skills. (This was especially important to me as I hoped the takeaway for the participants would be a true partnership—something that was missing when I first moved back to Florida.)

When I worked in the Developmental Disabilities Program of the Florida Department of Children and Families, I provided a family voice in decisions that impacted service delivery. I often spoke of the importance of communication with families and was honored to be asked by Governor Jeb Bush to write a bi-weekly bulletin to keep families informed of the progress being made during a redesign of the developmental disabilities program. Later, I had an opportunity to work as a consultant providing training on person-centered care for the staff of state institutions in Montana as they worked to move people back into their home communities.

Happily retired for several years, I floundered when, while in his late thirties, Matt got a diagnosis of Alzheimer's disease. As devastating as that news was, it led me to some of the most passionate people I have had the pleasure of knowing. Through the National Task Group on Intellectual Disabilities and Dementia Practices (NTG), I co-founded an online national support group for families who care for someone with an intellectual disability and dementia and have helped several organizations establish support groups in their state or local communities. About the same time, I created a social media support group for people who care for individuals aging with Down syndrome and diagnosed with Alzheimer's disease.

I feel I have had an amazing professional life that was filled with many opportunities. And I believe I have been more successful in every job I took on because Matt continued to teach me and inspire me. And give me strength!

My Baywatch Dream

These past few years, while fulfilling, have been difficult. Over 40 years ago, I became a support parent, ready to share our experiences having a young one with Down syndrome. It always felt incredible to offer guidance, encouragement, hope, and joy to families who had new babies sporting that extra chromosome. I have loved watching little ones, whose families entered my world, grow into teens and young adults ready to make an impact in whatever way they could. Now, I support families who are on a journey with an Alzheimer's diagnosis.

Caregiving changes when Alzheimer's enters our world.

Instead of a bright future, we face losses. We watch as our sons and daughters, our sisters and brothers, lose skills they worked so hard to achieve. We focus our efforts on keeping life upbeat and positive. As others come into our lives to help support and care for our loved ones, we work diligently to teach them who our family member was before dementia began to rob them of themselves. Not long ago, the reality of this supporting effort ripped a chunk of my heart when I learned that another family I had supported lost their loved one to Alzheimer's. This is the hardest part of supporting families, but it is also the part that keeps me motivated to continue. Every week there is another family grasping for a lifeline. I, and others like me, will be there to support, to care, and to share tears when the time comes.

It felt natural to get back to family advocacy work after several years of retirement. I must say that these past years are probably the most rewarding of my entire career. As a leader in the NTG, I learned of some medical professionals who were experts in Down syndrome. When I saw that one particular doctor would be in Orlando at a parent conference, I registered for my first Down syndrome convention in over thirty-five years. Dr. Brian Skotko, a physician who directs a Down syndrome clinic at Massachusetts General Hospital in Boston, was scheduled to have three workshops and I wanted to meet him.

I wasn't disappointed as he stood before his audience and shared that he was not only a medical geneticist, but that he also had a sister with Down syndrome. I don't recall the details of all the sessions he gave, but in his last one, he shared stories from a book he had co-authored.

One of those stories was of a young man who wanted to travel to California to meet the stars of Baywatch (a television series popular from the late 1980s through the early 2000s). He read passages of how the young man, despite his family not believing in his dream, was able to search the internet and put together a plan to make it a reality. This young fellow found the beach where filming was done; he found a hotel nearby; he even determined the airline flights needed to get to California. When he made it

to the beach, the stars were not there. But staff from the show were there and after he introduced himself, it was arranged for him to visit the set and watch some filming. His dream had come true, and he had worked hard to make it happen.

When the Orlando conference ended and I drove out of the congested traffic of the city, I saw mile after mile of palm trees and billboards. Driving in the right-hand lane of the interstate, cars to the left of me zipped by on the way to whatever urgent thing awaited them. I was not in the same hurry. I was thinking about the happy faces I had seen at the registration table where families greeted people they hadn't seen since the last year's conference. I had eavesdropped on conversations of parents leaving a session and talking about how they would use the information they had just learned to get a service their child desperately needed in school. It was a wonderful feeling knowing that so many families had been helped in those previous two days.

The drive across Interstate 4 from Orlando to Clearwater gave me a couple of hours to think. Most of the families at the conference had young children, and the experts and resources for their needs were rich and abundant. The farther I drove, the more troubled I felt that there wasn't anything like that for families of adults with Down syndrome. Since Matt's birth, there had been a significant increase in the expected life span of people with Down syndrome. Unfortunately, the literature and resources were slow to keep up with our loved ones' needs.

It didn't make sense to me. After all, there are many changes when our kids grow up and leave public school. I thought back on the days after Matt had finished school. Gone were the protections of a federal education law that applied to children in the public school system. After graduation, his supports came through the more limited options of the state program serving adults with developmental disabilities. It took a lot of energy to ensure he got and kept the services he needed. Gone were the pediatricians who knew so much about little ones with Down syndrome. Matt now saw medical providers who had large practices, and he was often the only person with Down syndrome seen in that clinic. As I drove across Florida, I couldn't let go of my thoughts.

And then it hit me. I could organize a conference for Matt and other adults with Down syndrome to provide the same level of support and community as was offered to the young ones.

You could make this happen, Jadene, I thought. In years past, I had worked on a number of conferences, both state and national ones. I coordinated multi-day meetings and was responsible for securing locations, identifying speakers, and working with them prior to the conferences. I handled registration and post-event evaluations. I was right: I could make this happen.

My energy level increased ten-fold as the possibilities evolved over miles of driving. As I pulled into my driveway, I felt a level of excitement I hadn't experienced before. I knew a conference of this type could be huge and be an important event for many people. For the next few weeks, as I sat in my studio, I played with those thoughts and then I got scared. I started thinking of all the time that had passed since I had done anything even remotely like this. I let doubt creep in, only to find myself periodically returning to the dream of a conference.

I dubbed it "My Baywatch Dream" and concluded that if a young man with Down syndrome could figure out how to get to California, I could figure out how to create a conference for adults with Down syndrome and their families.

"Let's Do This!"

I resolved to make it happen.

I sent emails to Florida Down syndrome associations and shared my idea with a small number of people. I couldn't let go of the dream and kept gathering the strength I needed to put the idea out into the universe. Although my original dream was for a Florida-based conference, I realized that I would like to have the support of my colleagues in the NTG. In early June 2017, Joe and I traveled in our RV, headed to the American Academy of Developmental Medicine and Dentistry (AADMD) conference in Houston. I was to present a session on family support and receive the NTG Spirit award at the conference. On our way, I sent one more email—to the co-chairs of the NTG, Matt Janicki and Seth Keller.

The NTG Steering Committee was going to gather the Sunday morning following the conference to discuss plans for the upcoming year. I thought it would be prudent to let them know what I had in mind, and that I would like to have their support for my dream conference. In less than an hour I received a reply from Matt who loved my idea and suggested that we meet with Sara Weir, who was also attending the conference. I had no idea who Sara was. As it turned out she was the president and CEO of the National Down Syndrome Society, a fact I did not know, because I had not been involved with any Down syndrome groups since Matt was a teen.

Joe and I arrived in the Houston area two days before the conference was to begin. The closest RV park was about a thirty-minute drive from the event hotel located in downtown Houston. We decided that I would stay at the hotel, and he would stay in the RV with our little dog. The afternoon prior to the start of the conference, we unhitched our tow vehicle (our 2007 VW Rabbit) and drove through heavy traffic. With a quick goodbye kiss, Joe dropped me off at the entrance to the hotel. The next couple of days were filled with typical conference activities. And then Saturday morning arrived.

Is there a real difference between anticipation and anxiety, I wondered as I exited the elevator. On my way to the breakfast meeting, thoughts tumbled around in my head so quickly I could only glimpse them for a moment.

Why is it so cold in here? Why do I need a jacket, scarf, and gloves to sit in a hotel meeting room? It costs a lot of money to keep it cold.

Stop it, Jadene, focus on what you are going to say.

You better choose your words carefully, so this Sara gal doesn't think you are crazy.

What a confusing design for a carpet. Circles and triangles and squares and too many colors. It hurts my eyes to look at it.

Pay attention—focus on what you're going to tell Sara.

Coffee! Short line. Great.

A conference, remember, it's all about a conference.

Grr. Why don't those people move and stir their beverage away from the coffee station?

OK, focus! How are you going to start your story?

Nice! Ooh, sausage, and eggs—no time for that. Hotel food smells so good yet tastes so strange? Why is that?

Should I tell the whole story about the conference in Orlando?

Should I just jump right into what I want to do?

Should I tell her about Matt first and why I even thought of this conference?

My stomach tightened; my palms began to sweat.

Oh, my, there they are!

I took a big breath and put an even bigger smile on my face.

"Good morning, Jadene," Seth said.

And so it began.

I told Sara about the Orlando conference and my Baywatch Dream. Before I could finish, she exclaimed, "Jadene, this is brilliant! I can't believe this hasn't been thought of before. Let's do this!"

I was shocked and thrilled. We spent the next half-hour discussing how we could make it happen. I was only slightly worried when she informed me that it was her plan to piggyback this new event on the NDSS Buddy Walk on Washington® already scheduled for the next Spring. I agreed to chair the conference, as she did not have staff available to take on a project of this size.

In April 2018, several hundred self-advocates, their families and people who support them gathered in Arlington, Virginia, for the very first Down Syndrome Adult Summit. That summit continues now. And I am happy to say that the National Down Syndrome Society has recognized that there needs to be more than a couple of days each year that focuses on adults.

It is an honor to have been hired to help guide that great organization in the development of programs that address young adults and those aging with Down syndrome, as well as their caregivers. I never dreamed I would be employed as I move toward my mid-seventies, but I was!

I am honored to have been recognized with the NTG Spirit Award in 2017 and with a National Down Syndrome Society Champion of Change Award in 2019. Over the years I have been blessed to receive a number of awards. Receiving them is nice, however, they are not the incentive for my work. As I come to the final chapters of my life, I am thrilled to know that by sharing what was in my heart, I have made a difference for families walking alongside and behind me. Every day I wake up grateful for the opportunities I continue to have. I'm especially thankful that Matt has shared his life with me, taught me valuable lessons and helped me grow stronger in many ways.

Spiritual Strength

Looking at Troubling Times

In addition to strengthening my skills personally and professionally, I recognize how I have grown stronger spiritually, as well. I have always felt that a person's faith and spirituality are private, between themselves and their God. When Matt was just a few weeks old, I got a phone call from someone I didn't know—a mother of a four-year old boy with Down syndrome. My mother had met her and asked that she give me a call. As we talked, she told me I had been blessed because my baby was a gift from God. I can still remember being uncomfortable hearing that and thinking that I could do without gifts of that nature—even though I loved Matt dearly. I struggled with that concept for many years because I had always believed in God, having been raised in the Presbyterian church. But I could never understand why God would subject anyone to a life that wasn't complete. I know now that I had a lot of learning to do!

At that time, I struggled. I couldn't comprehend why God would give me this pain or why He would ruin my life forever. It made no sense to me.

I had been away from my church for several years but knew that I wanted my boys to grow up with a church family. Living in Fort Benning, Georgia when Matt was a toddler, I found a church in Columbus and took the boys with me one Sunday morning. During the service, Matt made the noises and sounds we had come to expect since he had few spoken words. People stared at us; I smiled at them—but no one came to welcome us. I didn't go back. Over the years, I tried other churches in different cities where we lived. And, every time, it was the same. So, for a while, I just turned off the spiritual part of me.

While we lived in Germany, my friend Doug and I would sometimes talk about our lives and the paths we were on. We discussed what I thought was the reason I had a son with a disability; we talked about spirituality and how it played a part in our lives. Our discussions led me to visit the Stars and Stripes bookstore in search of books that would help me recognize the meaning of my life. I'm not sure I ever discovered that, but I did come up with a belief system that fits me. I will forever be grateful to Doug, who helped me find a connection to my God once again.

When we first returned from Germany, I easily remembered those conversations with Doug. I read—actually, I devoured—books on spirituality and found myself drawn to a Metaphysical approach to my beliefs. While the challenges Matt faced were daunting, I tried to meet his needs and attempted to keep balance in my family and my work, and I found myself slowly drifting away from God, once again. There was no energy, no time left to give or to think. Occasionally, I found myself saying a silent prayer for strength, or wisdom, or patience. But I didn't have much faith that they were being heard. Those were years of great struggle for me.

The good news is that the foundation I had built through those long conversations with Doug stayed with me, and when life settled a bit, I would buy another book and, once again, contemplate the mysteries of life. I have found that when I most need the strength that comes with a spiritual connection to my higher self and to God, my life creates the space for it to occur.

As I write, our world is struggling to get through the COVID-19 pandemic. It certainly has changed the way we live and interact.

One positive outcome from this new lifestyle for me has been the ability to reconnect with a friend. I was invited to participate in the online course led by my friend who was living in New York. I met Dr. Paula Petry shortly after we moved to Florida in the mid-eighties when we were both selected to serve on the Board of Directors for the newly created state-wide family support program, Parent to Parent of Florida. Within a few

years, she and I were consultants for Parent to Parent, supporting families in Florida as they established local groups around the state. I enjoyed conversations with Paula as she seemed to have an incredibly interesting life. I was always intrigued that she had a degree in Anthropology.

Paula had a little girl who was born with spina bifida. Alex was a little pixie—cute, sassy, and delightful. In the summer of 1996, Alex had a surgery related to spina bifida. Unfortunately, there were complications, and she died just days after her twelfth birthday. It is not unexpected that Paula lost herself in grief and she trekked many paths in her attempt to heal from her incredible loss. During her journey to healing, she received a Ph.D. in education. Not surprising to me, her explorations led her to study energy medicine, sound healing, mindfulness, and somatic therapies. Her work with Peruvian Shamans prompted her to find new ways to support parents of children with disabilities.

Despite our bond, we had lost touch over the years. I missed our conversations and never stopped thinking of her as a great friend. However, I was fortunate to reconnect with her in the Spring of 2020 when she was doing a Women's Summit at a Florida family and disability conference that was online due to restrictions in place from the COVID pandemic. Paula shared with me how the work she had done after Alex's death brought her to help parents heal when dealing with their child's disability. I am grateful for the discoveries I have made through our conversations and continue to make as I apply what I have learned from her. Every week, as I put into practice what she has taught me, I have found more peace and greater strength to plow through the difficult days I encounter.

This gift of spiritual growth has given me strength through many rough periods. Because of this gift, I can look at troubling times differently. My spiritual strength hasn't stopped difficult times. Those periods can still be hard to get through, but I am now able to pull away momentarily and know that somewhere in the pain is a new opportunity to learn, to grow, and to be strong.

I Have Chosen to Grow Stronger

Over the years, I have gained strength in several ways and, as a result, I have been able to help Matt shape a life that has meaning and brings great joy to both of us. This gift of strength—a gift that I didn't initially recognize—has been an important one in many parts of my life. Though not always easy, I have chosen to grow stronger at every opportunity!

Through the years I have:

- Tackled the unknown, whether it was a law, or a new beginning, and have gained strength personally.

- Explored and questioned the status quo and have experienced increased strength professionally.

- Challenged my religious beliefs and discovered amazing strength in my spirituality.

My Gift to You

Growing and gathering strength can happen when we least expect it to. I'm not sure I would have gained the strength I did had I not been supporting Matt. Strength comes by adapting to difficult situations—finding another way around a problem. We gain strength when we are proactive, look at challenges and think of what we could do differently. And strength comes by learning from our experiences. Building strength can take work, but it is worth the time and effort. Take a moment to reflect on your life and the strength you have.

1. What event in your life would you identify as a time that helped you grow stronger?

    _____

    _____

    _____

2. How have you used that strength in your life?

    _____

    _____

_____

_____

3. If there is an area in your life that you would like to have more strength, what could you do to promote that growth?

_____

_____

_____

A GIFT OF FRIENDSHIP

Dear Matt,

What a wonderful gift you have given me! When you were first born, I felt alone in the world. Your grandmother had once said I should not have a second child, yet here you were, and you were going to need a lot of attention.

Friends did not understand what it took for me to care for and nurture you. Some of those friends walked away. I look back now and realize they were never meant to be friends for life. When they left, a door opened that led me to many people who did understand what your care involved. You helped me find people who thought as I did, people who valued all life and weren't afraid of the hard work needed to raise children with extra challenges.

Now, I have a support network that is filled with people from around the world—other moms who face the same sort of challenges we have, doctors who care for and about children and adults with Down syndrome, and many folks who have gentle, compassionate souls. These are the people you led me to. They love unconditionally, just as you do. These are the people who don't become bitter and don't hold a grudge when life doesn't go as they planned.

You, my sweet man, have taught me how to love without judgment and how to value a person just because they are a human being. Because you shared your life with me, I have friends and acquaintances who I know I can turn to when I need support, a hug, or just a smile.

Thank you for loving me and teaching me about the power of friendship—an important part of our lives.

Love,
Momma

A Gift of Friendship

"Friendship is born at that moment when one person says to another: 'What! You too? I thought that no one but myself . . .'"

C. S. Lewis, Author

In the mid-eighties, I was a board member of Parent to Parent of Florida. This group of kindred souls shared my passion for supporting families when a disability moved into their homes. At a break in one of our quarterly board meetings, several of us discussed the different relationships we have with others. In that conversation, we shared the hurt of friends who had lost their connection to us, as well as the friends that we never got to know. We talked of the people who support us in our lives, both day-to-day and over time.

105

Joanne Scaturro, a short Italian lady, has been called an ambassador of love; we thought of her as the female Leo Buscaglia. She could tell the best stories and was often called the Queen of Funny. Joanne was a social worker who didn't know a stranger and the board member representing the Florida Department of Education. She always had an open heart and open arms for the warmest hugs. During that conversation about relationships, Joanne called the people who support us our "Heart Network."

I always loved that concept of a Heart Network. When I think of a Heart Network, I picture a large net constructed of strands of various fibers. Those fibers are woven together in such a way that makes the net strong. If, in time, pieces of that net get frayed or break, we can mend that section or even replace it with new fiber. Our Heart Network is very much the same. The people who make it up are represented in the different fibers, and we become stronger as we weave our network together. We can even mend relationships or replace them if necessary.

Joanne helped us recognize that those closest to us are in the center of our Heart Network and may include a spouse or partner, parents, and our children. That core of our Heart Network may also include a close friend or siblings. These are the people we can always turn to when we need a shoulder to cry on, a hug, or to share our deepest thoughts, worries, and frustrations.

Joanne told us that in our Heart Network, there also are people who are close to us but are not those we turn to regularly. They may be the people who help us make decisions about our lives or the lives of our children with disabilities, such as teachers, service providers, physicians, and therapists. They have an important role in our life, but we may not be in touch with them daily or even weekly.

Our Heart Network even includes those who we don't know well, but interacting with them seems to help us feel better—perhaps the mail delivery person, or the lady at the quilt shop. In part of our Heart Network may be people whose names we don't even know, but they put a smile on our face when we see them, like the bagger at the grocery store, or the cashier at our favorite fast-food restaurant.

Our Heart Network is a part of our life that brings us support, comfort, and peace—and sometimes just a smile.

When I think of my Heart Network I realize how it has changed over time. For many years I have loved a quote I once saw on a Flavia Weedn greeting card. The first time I saw these words, I read them again and again.

Some people come into our lives and quickly go.

Some stay for a while, leave footprints on our heart

and we are never, ever the same.

My Heart Network—that strong interpersonal network I have had throughout Matt's life—has been filled with lots of footprints. I often think of the people I have crossed paths with, and those who have joined me for short and long distances on this journey of life. Let me explain.

When Matt was tiny, overcoming each little difficulty felt like ascending a steep and jagged mountain, and I was scaling that mountain alone. I had taken no lessons for this sort of challenge and often felt like I was climbing blindly. I knew no one who had a baby with Down syndrome, and for some time, I struggled with what I was supposed to do. I found myself doubting my ability to be a good mother to my new baby. With every attempt I made to climb higher up the mountain, I found more obstacles in my way. It seemed I would never reach the summit.

Connections

Matt was a good baby; he was difficult to feed, however. I was unsuccessful nursing him, so I contacted the La Leche League for help. As soon as the lady on the other end of the line heard me say that my baby had Down syndrome, she suddenly had to get off the phone. She promised to call me back, but that call never came. That was a connection lost before it could begin.

Unsuccessful with breastfeeding, I turned to bottle feeding. But even that proved frustrating as Matt had trouble latching onto those nipples as I attempted to feed him his formula. I was desperate to provide him with nourishment and experimented with every brand of baby feeding system that was popular during the mid-seventies. Even the bottle that claimed to be "most like mother, herself," didn't work. None of my friends understood the problem I was facing and had no advice or empathy to share with me. Connections weakened.

When Matt was about nine months old, I was invited to lunch with some girlfriends I had known for several years. My mother-in-law agreed to watch Michael for me but said that she was not comfortable keeping Matt as well. I checked with my mom and sister, but they were both working. So, Matt came with me.

I rode with my three friends to the mall in Merritt Island where we had lunch at the Piccadilly Cafeteria. There were a lot of people eating there when we arrived, but we were able to find a table where we could pull up a highchair for Matt's infant seat. As we sat eating, I began to realize that this wasn't just a girls' day out. My friends felt it was their responsibility to inform me that I spent too much time with Matt. In their eyes, I was neglecting

Matt in his infant carrier—the one he used when I was invited to lunch with girlfriends. Spring 1975, Brevard County, Florida

Michael and the evidence was right next to me in his infant carrier.

I felt betrayed. My heart ached and my appetite vanished. I wanted to run from that restaurant. But I couldn't leave. It became extremely uncomfortable for me as I listened to them tell me all the things I was doing wrong. I could not respond; I couldn't even speak as I listened to them go on and on in what felt like condemnation. They had no idea how disheartened I was; they had no idea how challenging it was trying to feed a baby who could not latch on to a nipple to suckle. This baby, sleeping quietly in that plastic carrier, was losing weight. No matter how much time we spent as he tried to eat, he never took enough formula to grow and gain even a few ounces. Still, as I write this, I feel the sadness I felt that day. I was truly alone, and those I thought I could count on didn't have a clue what my life had become—nor did they make the effort to even try to understand. And yet they judged me. Connections broken.

In time, I met some mothers who had children with Down syndrome or other intellectual disabilities. They became a lifeline for me. Finally, I had someone I could talk with about the challenges I faced. I didn't have to explain why I did the things I did, the worries I had, the guilt I felt, or why I didn't complete tasks that I had planned to do. Connections created.

The Arc is a national organization that supports people with intellectual and developmental disabilities, with chapters in every state and numerous communities. At that time, many of the members were the same parent pioneers who had started classes in church basements for their children with intellectual disabilities.

One of the earliest connections I made was with the Brevard County, Florida chapter of The Arc. After a phone conversation, they provided me with some print materials about babies with Down syndrome. When Matt was not quite three years old, we became a military family when Joe returned to the Army during an economic downturn. The Brevard Arc helped me connect with the chapter in Columbus, Georgia. This connection introduced us to families who could help us get settled and find services for Matt. Connecting with The Arc became a link to families in several of our moves.

Still, I found it difficult to make friends, even with those moms who were raising a child with a disability. Matt was always quite different from other little ones with Down syndrome. He began using a few words by the time he was two, and then stopped talking by the age of four. He had quirky little behaviors that seemed odd to people who didn't know him very well, and there were lots of stares from strangers out in public. As he lost the words he knew, he began making grunting and guttural sounds that were unexpected and often loud. People walked away from us. The circle of moms who stayed grew small. Connections never made.

Date Nights with Joe

Having couples as friends was also quite difficult. In 1977, when we moved to Georgia, I went back to school to get my bachelor's degree. For several years we moved from military to civilian life and back again. In the mid-eighties we left the military (or so I thought) and settled in our current home in west-central Florida. The Pinellas County Sheriff's Office hired Joe and he worked the midnight shift. His nights off were usually in the middle of the week. We had an almost teenage son with a disability—a son who had a lot of unusual behaviors and made lots of loud noises. It was during those years when his aggression and self-abuse increased, and it was impossible to find someone (other than Michael) to watch Matt for even a few hours.

I remember one evening when we got a woman to stay with Matt so we could attend a musical production of "Jesus Christ Superstar." She was an older lady who seemed a bit wary of Matt, and I was not totally comfortable leaving him with her. Worried about what he might be doing, it was quite difficult for me to relax enough to enjoy the performance. When we got home the sitter couldn't get out of the house quickly enough. Before she left, she ran through a litany of all that had gone wrong. "That boy refused to listen to me. He threw his stuffed animals, and he screeched loudly. He wouldn't go to bed when I told him to. He was just terrible and the most difficult child I have ever cared for."

111

My heart broke for Matt as I was certain that she had not attempted to do the things we suggested to help keep him calm. I felt sad—for myself and for Joe—as I realized we couldn't plan a single night out unless we made Michael (who was about sixteen at the time) be our childcare. It wasn't fair to Michael, to Matt, or to us.

Finding Myself

We started doing activities separately. Joe would play golf or go to the gun range with his deputy friends. I would have lunch or go out for coffee with the mothers in our support group. Most were much younger than me, and other than the disability connection, we had little in common.

Many years later, as I contemplated where I was in my life, I recognized that everyone I considered a friend was connected to me because of disability. I began to wonder if I had lost myself in this world. I reflected on that Flavia quote about footprints on our hearts and the conversation between the board members about the Heart Network that had occurred years before. I decided that I wanted to expand my world and began to examine the parts of me that had been smothered.

I remembered how much I used to love to sew and recalled the years when my wardrobe was filled with handmade creations. I wondered if that hobby could connect me to others with whom I could share time. So, I joined a local chapter of the American Sewing Guild and started attending meetings of two neighborhood groups. It was fun and fulfilling to have conversations that weren't centered around disability but focused on beautiful textiles and terms like "straight of grain," "width of fabric," pins, patterns, scissors, and pressing vs ironing. I became close to several of the women in these groups, and we started spending a lot of time together. I taught myself heirloom sewing techniques by attending classes online. For the first time in many years, I connected with ladies (and a few fellows) who shared my love of stitching beautiful things. Through sewing I found some new friends who became part of my Heart Network—friends who shared my hobby and really listened when I spoke about my struggles supporting an adult with a lifelong disability. With these new friends, I learned to piece quilts and began sewing for wonderful causes—children's clothing for families who were struggling, quilts for military veterans, and pillowcases for kids in the hospital. I had opened the door to a world that brought me joy and sparked my creativity.

Sometimes Forever is Not the People

I found myself wondering about the friends I had years before. I thought of all the people who had come into my life—and Flavia's quote resonated even more with me. Not long ago I came upon the work of Karen Salmansohn, a bestselling author who is passionate about empowering people to live their happiest, highest potential lives. She put into words something that I have believed for many years.

"We don't meet people by accident. They're meant to cross our path for a reason. If a relationship doesn't survive the test of time, it doesn't mean it still wasn't meant to be. Not all encounters with people are meant to last forever. Sometimes people are in our lives to teach us something. Sometimes the forever is not the person, but what we gain from them."

When I discovered those words, especially the last sentence, I realized how my Heart Network had included the people who left footprints on my heart and those who quickly left—some

113

even before they disturbed the dirt in the path. There were even some who stayed long enough to break things, rough things up, and trample on my heart and soul.

I now know that the people I get to meet all have a role to play in my life and I am grateful for each of them. I want to thank them all, even those who have made me angry, because that gave me an opportunity to clarify the principles by which I choose to live my life. I thank those who may have hurt me (intentionally or unintentionally) because they have helped me to know how I want to treat others.

I thank those people who have been friends for my lifetime, even if we don't see each other or talk very often. They have helped me solidify who I am. And there are a few people who have left deep footprints on my heart. They are the ones who have been steadfast for me, who have loved me and supported me even when I may not have been very loveable. They are the ones who have taught me to love myself. I cherish them.

Strength and Vulnerability

As I grow older, I find I spend more time reflecting on the people whose paths have crossed mine. It's a bit like a puzzle trying to figure out how it was we happened to meet and interact. I find comfort knowing that disability brought many of these people to me. They have come to me through Matt; they have shared some of the most difficult times in my life, and some of the sweetest moments.

Quite recently, reflections on my Heart Network revealed a painful truth: by being strong for everyone else, I kept a lot of people from coming too close. I focused on others' needs and not my own. I see now that some of my strength was built on a foundation of tears and fears. I spent years trying to prove I could do anything, that I was not vulnerable.

But I know now that I did not have to hide my vulnerability. I'm so glad that we are never too old to learn because I've discovered that I can be strong and vulnerable at the same time. I am not less effective because I sometimes need a shoulder to cry on. Knowing this about myself is opening a door to include more people in my Heart Network, and I am learning how to be more comfortable as I allow myself to share the thoughts imprinted on my heart.

Even with the knowledge that I have kept a distance with some people, I still feel extremely blessed. Sometimes I wonder how I got so lucky! I am protected by that network of supportive friends. And, just like a net is created from different lengths and various strengths of fibers, my support network is made of friendships in a variety of forms. Such comfort and safety I feel, knowing I have a strong Heart Network.

I am blessed to have a heart filled with footprints! In my Heart Network I have people who:

- Make me smile when I see the joy Matt brings to them.

- Care about Matt and see him and us occasionally.

- Let me call at any time to share my fears, my tears, my frustrations, and the silly things Matt has done.

My Gift to You

My Heart Network has often been a lifeline for me, especially in the difficult times. There have been times when only a dear friend in my Heart Network would understand the silliness/frustration/triumph of the stories I sometimes need to share. These friendships are some of the best gifts we are bestowed when our children have extra challenges in life.

Let's discover who is in your Heart Network. Acknowledge those people you have identified by putting their names in the heart on the next page.

Let your Heart Network support you, lift you up and be your lifeline when needed. At any time, you can add and remove people in your support system. Our hearts and lives are filled with wonderful people. Be open to let them in. Hold them close and invite them to join you as you walk this path of love, fear, joy, worry, uncertainty, and hope.

1. The person or persons who are closest in your Heart Network will be those who make you feel understood. They are the ones who really hear you. They know what you are saying even when you can't find the words. They are in the center of your Heart Network.

_____

_____

_____

_____

2. There are people in your Heart Network who help you from time to time. They might be the ones you go to with questions but may not need to rely on every day. They create the second level of your Heart Network.

_____

_____

_____

3. There are people you see only occasionally; even so, you know you can count on them for a pick-me-up. They are the people you encounter who can put a smile on your face or make you feel better, if just for a moment. They make up the outer level of your Heart Network.

_____

_____

_____

My Heart Network

A GIFT OF COMMUNICATION

Dear Matt,

I think every mother dreams of the day her child will say those four delightful words, "I love you, Mommy."

I have come to accept that I will never hear you say them. Knowing that has stung my heart. Speech has always been a challenge for you, but I have been blessed to know your voice because there have been times in your life that you were able to say some words.

I learned early in your life that even though you didn't say words, you understood what you heard. I also learned that you could speak to me in many other ways—through your smiles, by the way you waved your hands in excitement, or even by the way you gave me a thumb up or down. You showed me by taking ahold of my hand and leading me to whatever it was you wanted.

As I look back at our life together, I realize that some of your most difficult times happened because others could not hear your voice—no matter how hard you tried to communicate. Frustrating for me, I am sure it was even more so for you. I've watched as you were treated as if you were less than others when some people thought you had nothing to say. They certainly weren't listening! There are those who used to tell me that you couldn't communicate. We know that isn't true, don't we?

Without saying a word, you have shown me what is important.

When you squint your eyes tightly and tap your forehead with your fingers, I know that you have a headache. And when you sign "stop," and point to the store as I drive you home, I understand you want to go shopping (most likely for a new cat toy on a stick because those are your favorite). When you give me a thumb up, I know you like whatever I've said to you. And when you turn that thumb down, I know you don't want to do what I've suggested. Pizza always gets a thumb up and rice the opposite. A car ride or shopping: thumb up (sometimes two thumbs up). A love story on television: thumb down every time. I love that you have learned to video chat with me since the pandemic has kept us apart. Even though you only say a quick "hi," and wave when I answer your call, I know you are OK if you are smiling at me. I wonder what is bothering you if you have no sparkle in your eyes. When you turn your face away from the camera, it is clear that you are unhappy

with me. (I'm glad that doesn't happen very often.) When you sign "I love you," and blow me kisses, I know without a doubt that I'm in your heart as you are mine.

Without saying a word, you have spoken to me in countless ways.

My heart swells when we are together and, ever so gently, you brush your lips across the back of my hand. It's your silent way of saying, "I love you and thank you for what you do for me." Simply and beautifully, you have expressed gratitude. Every soft kiss is a reminder of the gentleness of your soul.

Without saying a word, you have taught me one of life's most important lessons.

Communication is through words **and** actions. It is through expressions, as well. I have accepted that I will never hear you say, "I love you, Momma." It's OK, because I know that you have told me that in countless ways. What a gift it has been to understand that even though you do not use words, you still have a lot to say.

Communication! I've learned so much about it because of you. And I thank you for that.

Love,
Momma

A Gift of Communication

"Nonverbal communication forms a social language that is in many ways richer and more fundamental than our words."

Leonard Mlodinow,
American Theoretical Physicist,
Screenwriter, and Author

How Naïve I Was

Matt was about two years old when we sold our home and moved to a rental property. The country was in a recession and Joe was unable to find a job after he graduated from college. So, he re-enlisted in the Army, and was off for training, while the boys and I waited in Florida.

The family across the street from our rental house had a grown son with an intellectual disability of some sort. He was a tall, thin man with dark hair. He often wandered around their front yard in the afternoon. As he paced back and forth across the lawn, ping-ponging between the tall palm trees, he made loud noises. I was a young mom, and he frightened me. I wasn't physically afraid of him; no, my fear came from something more terrifying. He represented what Matt's future could be. Would my little Matt, who was just beginning to say a few words, grow up to be like this man? Would he make loud noises that frightened people? Oh, how I hoped that wouldn't be the case. Little did I know the lessons that were ahead of me. When I reflect on those early days, I now understand how naïve I was.

I had been a particularly good English grammar student in school. I loved diagraming sentences and was troubled when people used words incorrectly. I'll admit now that I had a bit of grammar police in my blood. I believed good grammar was a sign of power and intelligence. Matt learned words slowly. By the time we had moved into the rental house, he had a small vocabulary. Although he was over two, he only used the typical first words most babies say, "momma," "dada," and "bobba" for his bottle. I was pleased that he was learning to talk, especially since the words were so hard gained.

Just a few months before his third birthday we made that move to Fort Benning, Georgia. I was excited when I learned there was a developmental center for preschoolers that he could attend in Columbus. Even so, it was difficult putting Matt in the little green Army van every morning. He was still quite tiny. Matt was totally dependent on me for everything. He had taken his first steps just a few short weeks before he started attending the center and still could not walk far before he was too tired

124

to continue. Every morning, he toddled to the van, and then I carried him up the steps because they were higher than he could lift his little legs. Even though Matt smiled as I strapped him in his car seat and kissed the top of his head, there were tears those first few days—mine.

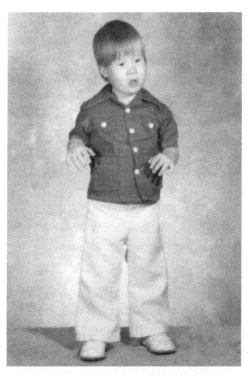

Matt stood and took his first steps just before his third birthday. Fort Benning, Georgia

A little more than a year later, I was learning to fight for him. My little boy who just months before was gaining new words had stopped talking. Instead, he grunted and made other noises that weren't words, just sounds. Filled with confusion, I took him out of the developmental center. I felt a bit of anger towards the staff. The other children with Down syndrome were progressing and he wasn't. I wondered if the staff was really working with him; whatever they were doing wasn't enough. By then, I had begun studying child development and knew that the early years were critical to his brain growth. I began to feel anxious that Matt was losing precious time, and somehow found the Portage Project Infant/Toddler Assessment and Curriculum from the University of Wisconsin. That blue vinyl case filled with cards for all sorts of developmental skills was a source of hope for me. Using this curriculum, I began teaching Matt at home. That kit gave me insight into not only what Matt should be doing each month, but also how to help him learn. Even as his ability to talk was diminished, I began to learn more about communication as I worked with him every day.

I loved watching Matt as he discovered the names of objects like spoon, ball, puppy, book. He made no attempt to repeat those words to me but each time I asked him to point to an object he got it correct. I knew he was learning and continued to hope that his speech would come later.

The Use of Words Came and Went

The Muscogee County school district had a kindergarten program for children with intellectual disabilities who weren't being served elsewhere. Because Matt had attended the developmental center, they said he wasn't eligible for their program. (At that time, the federal law was interpreted that a child under five, receiving services in a community program was not entitled to a public-school program.) I knew it was important that Matt be in school where he could receive the therapies he needed. I pushed back and the administrators eventually relented. Matt was enrolled in the Trainable Mentally Handicapped Kindergarten class at Wynnton Elementary School. (I have chosen to write in the terminology as it was used in the period we were living because I believe it helps to explain some of the low expectations people had for children with Down syndrome when Matt was little.)

From everything I had been told to expect by the doctors and other professionals who had assessed or treated Matt, I was not surprised by the placement that he was given.

During that era when I was learning about fighting for Matt's rights, I enrolled in Columbus College to continue my education. It had become quite clear to me that anything I shared about Matt with professionals was ignored because I was just his mom. They did not see the value of my point of view even though I had spent thousands of hours with Matt, acutely tuned in to how he talked, played, listened, and worked so hard to understand us. One of the classes in the curriculum for a degree in special education was educational psychology. As we studied abnormal psychology (seriously?), I learned about Autism. And as I read through the signs of that developmental disability, I recognized Matt. He had language and then lost it; he had several repetitive behaviors; he had no interest in his toys.

Education classifications in the late seventies included:

Educable Mentally Handicapped (EMH):
students are capable of mastering basic vocational skills and can learn to read and write.

Trainable Mentally Handicapped (TMH):
students are capable of learning personal hygiene and other living skills in a sheltered setting, such as a group home.

Profoundly Mentally Handicapped (PMH):
students are unable to independently care for themselves without ongoing significant assistance from a caregiver throughout adulthood.

By the time he started kindergarten, he was not using any words and was exhibiting worrisome, repetitive behaviors. Hour after hour Matt would hold a piece of paper close to his face, flicking it with his index finger. When I was determined that behavior needed to stop, and I took the cards and papers away so he wouldn't flip them, he changed his actions up a little. He then started tapping his finger on the bridge of his nose and scraping it with his fingernail until his nose was raw, sometimes bleeding. I realized pretty quickly that I needed to be careful about how I dealt with Matt's unusual behaviors. I had stopped something that was annoying to me but not at all harmful and my action ended up creating a more difficult behavior. While I could take away a card or piece of paper, I couldn't take away his little fingers.

Matt was enrolled at Wynton Elementary School in 1979 where Barbara Rouse was his teacher. Columbus, Georgia

I still believed that Matt could learn to speak, and so did his kindergarten teacher, Barbara Rouse. Barbara was a young mom who had tremendous energy. She was thin, blonde and had a smile that was contagious. We quickly became friends as we worked together to help Matt. (I was fortunate to do my student teaching under her guidance and learned so much from her that helped Matt and many others.) Barbara explained to me that the school's speech therapist had suggested that we use total communication with Matt. She had seen some great results with little ones with Down syndrome using signs as a visual cue with the spoken word. I was on board immediately. We soon noticed that as Matt learned signs, he also began making approximations for the words. We were encouraged.

128

However, at the same time, Matt was seeing a speech therapist privately, outside of school. He was an older gentleman, very paternalistic in his approach to therapy; he was adamant that signs would make Matt lazy, and that he would stop trying to speak. I don't recall how long we took Matt to this therapist, but I do remember that I spoke with Barbara and the speech therapist at the school about the recommendation to not use signs. Together we decided that in all settings other than with the outside therapist, we would continue with the total communication approach. It was just one of the times that I had to sort through the conflicting information I was being given, and hope that I was making the right decision for Matt.

Over the years, Matt's spoken vocabulary grew to nearly 100 words (or approximations for words). I held out hope that one day he would be able to carry on a conversation with me, and still dreamed of the day he would say, "I love you, Mommy." Matt's words were not clear; some sounded like English ("cah" for car, bye-bye, and "Maa" for his own name) while others were of his own inventions. He said "wookie" when he wanted to listen to music, and "peepaw" for pizza. He certainly had his own language.

Some years later, Joe received military orders to Germany where Matt was enrolled in a German residential school the last year we were there. Since most of Matt's language was his own creation, I was a worried momma because I knew that the staff, who did not speak English, would not understand what he was trying to say. I struggled with how he would communicate with the people in his home and school, and finally decided to make a list of all the words he used. I created three columns; in the first column was the word as Matt said it; the second column was what the word was in English; the third column was the

German translation of his word. The staff at the school and his home were grateful to have the *Dictionary of Matt* so they could understand him when he attempted to communicate.

Matt's use of words came and went throughout his childhood and into his teen years. Matt was about twelve years old when we came home to Florida at the end of Joe's tour in Germany. We tried to teach Matt to communicate using a clunky piece of equipment about the size of a shoebox. We put printed pictures on it and then recorded words that he might say. For example, he could press the picture of pizza and it would say (in his momma's voice), "I want some pizza, please." He liked the device—as a toy. I could never get him to use it to ask for things he wanted. He played with it, touching the same picture over and over and over. I finally sent the device back to the state program that had loaned it to him. Later, we tried using the letter board that seemed to be effective for students who are Autistic. That consisted of a laminated, printed keyboard that was placed in front of him. His teacher or speech therapist would support his arm near his elbow. He would then type out the words to answer questions or ask for something. It made me think of a Ouija board. Was it working or was his hand being manipulated to spell words? Matt didn't even know how to read, so how could he know how to spell? We got favorable reports from the school, however, when I tried it with him at home, I got nothing. I asked that the use of facilitated communication be stopped.

Once again, I felt frustrated. I was filled with questions and feelings of inadequacies. Was Matt willing to do something for his teachers that he refused to do with me? Were the teachers anticipating how Matt would answer because they knew him well enough to know what he would say if he could? Or was I not assisting Matt correctly causing him to just sit and not respond?

I never found answers to those questions so I kept doing what I could to understand what my son was trying to say.

At age sixteen he had a seizure, and he began to take medication to prevent more of them. Within a year he had lost all the words he was using (which weren't a lot). I was heartbroken, but felt his health was more important than his ability to talk. Over the ensuing years, Matt has spoken a few words but not enough for effective communication. He never lost, "Momma," and "Maa," and I cherish the "I love you," sign he uses to convey what he can't verbalize.

Matt's limited communication has been one of the hardest parts of my life as his mom. Never hearing, "I love you," has been tough, but that's not what is most difficult. It has been the uncertainly of whether I was doing what Matt would choose for his life. I like to think that I know my son. Except for the time he spent in the residential school, I spent the first twenty-four years of his life with him nearly every day and every night. Still, I found myself questioning decisions I made for him.

A mom doesn't always know. Even with my son Michael, who had none of Matt's challenges with communication, I was surprised by a big decision he made. He and I had a special connection as he grew up. When he was in high school, he would come into my room to chat with me when he got home from a night out with his friends. Yet, I was caught off-guard in his senior year when he announced he was going to take the ASVAB (Armed Services Vocational Aptitude Battery) exam. He had made plans to join the U.S. Coast Guard. I was not prepared for his decision and was a bit flabbergasted because I thought I knew everything about him.

Guessing What Matt Wanted

Now please understand, I hadn't had those same long conversations with Matt. I was always guessing what Matt wanted or liked based on the reactions he had to the things we had exposed him to or the things he experienced in school. I know that Matt loves pizza by the amount he consumes, asking for a second, third, or even a fourth piece when it is served. He won't let me put rice or peas on his plate. That tells me a lot. He loves action-filled movies like *Twister* (that he has watched so much we have replaced the DVD at least a half dozen times). He doesn't like watching Hallmark movies with me but would watch a war movie with his dad. Repeatedly, throughout Matt's life I have second-guessed decisions I've made, even though I know him intuitively. Confirmation that I'm getting it right is what I have continually sought.

In Florida, students in exceptional education programs can stay in school through to the age of twenty-one. So, when Matt was twenty years old, I started thinking seriously about his life after school. I had the opportunity to participate with Matt in a future planning process with Vicky Barnitt, a friend who facilitated P.A.T.H. sessions. Planning Alternative Tomorrows with Hope is a tool that was created by Jack Pearpoint, Marsha Forrest, and John O'Brien in Canada to help individuals with disabilities, their families and those who support them to create a positive future. P.A.T.H. reverses the planning process, starting with the big dream for the future—the North Star—and works backward to create an action plan that can begin immediately. I had watched Vicky guide the development of a P.A.T.H. at a family conference and was eager to do one for Matt.

One afternoon, about a year before Matt left school, Vicky came to our home and taped an exceptionally large sheet of paper on

our living room wall. It was there that she would document in words and colorful graphics our dreams for Matt's future. Joe and I had invited our friend Christa Brown and Matt's classroom aid, Ted, to help us create his P.A.T.H. I wished Michael had been with us, but he was stationed in Washington state with the U. S. Coast Guard.

I had met Christa several years earlier when she arrived at a party with Michael. I was quite surprised when she immediately ran to Matt and was so excited to see him. It turned out she had been a volunteer in Matt's school and had known him for more than a year. Christa became family, and she frequently included Matt in activities. She even took Matt to his school proms the last two years he was there. Matt seemed to enjoy spending time with Christa and was quite happy when she told me that I could not go with them to his last prom. When she told me that Matt deserved to have a date night he looked at me with a big grin and gave Christa a thumb up!

Ted had worked with Matt for several years, and Matt always responded in a positive way when Ted was around. In 1994, Ted helped Matt when he was the Best Man in Michael's first wedding that was held in our backyard. Joe and I felt that Ted understood Matt and would have some ideas about what he might want in his life after he left school.

I rearranged the furniture in the living room so that we were all facing the wall that would soon contain the vision for Matt's future. Joe and I sat in chairs I had brought from the dining room table to the right of Vicky. Ted and Matt had taken their seats on the sofa. Christa sat in one of the other chairs from the dining room. We chatted for a few minutes, catching up with each other's activities.

And then Vicky took the cap off one of the scented markers and smiled. "What does Matt want in his future? It can be anything, whether it seems possible or not," she began.

In the P.A.T.H. process, Matt was the "focus person." Vicky's question was one I had reflected on for many years so I thought I knew what Matt wanted. Yet I sat paralyzed, unable to speak. I was afraid to say out loud what I had considered Matt's future to look like. In my heart, I knew that I was about to make a huge commitment by putting words to my thoughts, and those words would get captured on the gigantic blank page in front of us. I knew I would then be accountable to make it happen, and that scared me—what if I couldn't do it? What if I just gave up? Everyone in the room would know I had let Matt down.

So, I sat, without saying a word. No one else spoke either.

Vicky asked the question again, and I broke the silence with silliness. "All the pizza he can eat!" I exclaimed.

Everyone laughed as Vicky drew a picture of pizza on the paper, and we proceeded to create a vision for the life we thought Matt would love, his North Star Dream. It took us nearly three hours to complete the process. Our work covered what Matt could have in a few years, right down to the tasks I could work on immediately to put this dream into motion. As we discussed Matt's future, he sat cross-legged on the sofa. Hour after hour Matt held a stick from the oak tree in our front yard close to his face, twitching it back and forth. He may have grunted a couple times but seemed totally disengaged from what we were doing. I was sad because I believed we had created a future that I imagined for Matt and doubted that we had captured what he really wanted for his life.

The final part of the planning process is when the facilitator reads the P.A.T.H. back to the focus person. Vicky pointed out all the steps we would take to reach goals that were set for the next year and more. Then she reached the North Star Dream and told Matt that his parents and friends saw him living in a home of his own with a flower garden and all the pizza he wanted to eat. I still was unsure that Matt cared about what we had just done.

But then, Matt jumped up from the sofa and threw his arms in the air. That sudden movement and gesture of excitement clearly showed us that he did indeed understand, was paying attention, and approved! Once again, without saying a word, Matt communicated, this time in a large and exuberant way. It was me who now sat silently. Tears streamed down my face, and I mirrored the same joyous smile as Matt's.

That evening, as I helped Matt with his bath, I decided he needed to learn to do more of his own self-care. I squeezed a small amount of shampoo on his wet head. I then told him to wash

The first P.A.T.H. we did for Matt as we attempted to figure out what his life might be like after public school. Spring 1995, Clearwater, Florida

his hair and showed him what I meant by making the motions of shampooing on my own head. He looked at me like I was speaking a foreign language and made no attempt to even lift his arms from the warm bath water. Three times I prompted him and modeled the behavior I was seeking. Three times I got the same blank stare. By then, I was aggravated and exasperated. In frustration, I warned him, "Matt, if you ever want to leave home and not have mommy telling you what to do, you have to wash your own hair."

Suddenly, water went everywhere as his hands flew to his head and he scrubbed and scrubbed. I didn't know whether to laugh or cry. My kid had been playing the poor little disabled child and I had fallen for it. And then I had a twinge of heartbreak as I realized he really did want to move away. My baby boy had grown up.

As I have been writing this book, our family has suffered a huge loss. For the past several years, Joe had been in declining health, and I worried a lot when the world first learned about the COVID-19 pandemic. In February 2021, Joe was hospitalized with pneumonia (his second hospitalization for pneumonia in only a few months). I was happy when he came home after eight days—even though he had a lot of home health services that were necessary to help him continue to heal. Just one week later, he left the house on a stretcher and was diagnosed with COVID. For twelve long, grueling days and nights he fought but didn't have the strength to battle a virus that attacked his weakened lungs. The afternoon Joe died, Kandie Warner and Pastor Joyce Stone, from Matt's church, went to Matt's home where they told him about his dad. Kandie and Joyce did a remarkable job sharing the terrible news and when they finished, Matt signed, "Dad," "Jesus," "Heaven," and "heart." Kandie said she had told him that

his daddy died and was with Jesus in Heaven and would be in his heart forever. Matt shared those signs at the celebration of life we held in his church a few weeks later, and even now, several months since Joe died, Matt will sign "Dad," and "Heaven," or "Dad," and "Heart." That man definitely knows how to communicate!

By the way, when Matt was in his thirties, the psychiatrist acknowledged what I had known since he was a toddler. That doctor put into words what all the professionals before him believed could not be. Children with Down syndrome can have Autism. The behaviors Matt experienced were not because he has Down syndrome but because he is also Autistic with Apraxia (a speech disorder that results from difficulty moving the muscles of the mouth and tongue needed to form words). It is comforting to know that most doctors now understand that there can be a dual diagnosis, for kids with Down syndrome who also fall somewhere on the Autism spectrum.

I Don't Have to be Afraid of What I Don't Know

I still have the P.A.T.H. that we completed that afternoon so many years ago. I love to look at it and see all that we have helped Matt to accomplish. He lives in St. Petersburg, Florida in a home that he rents with another gentleman. The landlord bought the house specifically for Matt and made sure that he has a pool because he loves being in the water, laughing and splashing. Matt is no longer interested in gardening so having flowers hasn't been a part of his life for some time. He worked as a volunteer at the Bay Pines Veterans Administration Health Care System for over nine years until COVID put everyone in lockdown. We are still trying to decide when might be a good time for him to return to that job that he loved.

As I look back over our life together, I feel a little embarrassed that I was frightened by the man who lived across the street from us when I was a young mother. Matt helped me learn that I don't have to be afraid of what I don't know. I've come to realize that nonverbal communication *is* communication. I've known that tone of voice, facial expressions and body language play a big part in our communications. Unfortunately, it took me a long time to realize that Matt and I have all of that, we just don't share the spoken words. I know he understands whatever I say to him.

I have found comfort in learning that I communicate in an extremely special way with Matt. I marvel at how much Matt has taught me in his forty-eight years. Communication happens in many ways—yes with our voices, but it happens in other ways that can actually be more impactful. A look, a gesture, an action, can all convey messages that are heard with the heart.

With few words, Matt had led me to where he wanted to be in his life. I learned some tremendous lessons that day we created his P.A.T.H.:

- Matt pays attention to what's going on, even when he seems disengaged.

- I know Matt, and he trusts me to make decisions that are in his best interest.

- We don't need words to communicate effectively.

My Gift to You

Even when we can use words to communicate, much is said through our nonverbal communications. Facial expressions, body language, gestures, and touch are all ways to communicate without words. In fact, nonverbal communication is almost as important as verbal responses—in some cases, more. Nonverbal communication is a satisfying way to interact when we realize just how powerful it is.

1. Think about ways that people communicate without using words. List them below.

   _____

   _____

   _____

2. What can you do to improve your nonverbal communication?

   _____

   _____

   _____

3. Think of a specific person in your life and the unique connection you have. What is one way you could let them know that you love them without using words?

_____

_____

_____

A GIFT OF GRATITUDE

Dear Matt,

I gave birth to you, but you gave birth to a family advocate. I had a lot to learn when I accepted the role to champion your rights, and I have never regretted a minute of the hard work it has taken.

Learning to speak up for you meant that I had to recognize what you needed. But I also had to know what moms had already done for their children with Down syndrome. Without being acquainted with their history, I would have had to start from the beginning. But the "Momma Bears" (and some "Poppa Bears") that came before me had built a road for us to travel, and it was being paved when you were a baby.

Those mommas and daddies started classes for their children when their kids weren't allowed to attend school with their brothers, sisters, or neighbors. And do you know what else they did, Matt? They got laws written so all children with disabilities could attend public school. And they helped write laws to bring children who had been placed in large institutions back home to live in their communities.

Matt, we were fortunate to have had those strong mommas and daddies work so hard before you were born and when you were little. They started a movement with a message that we still work on today: people with disabilities have the same value and worth as every other human being.

What they did was just the beginning of the human rights story that you have helped write every day of your incredible life. You and the kiddos who follow you remind us that everyone has something to contribute to our world.

So, Matt, now I want to thank you for giving me the gift of gratitude for the mommas and daddies that came before me. Thank you for opening my eyes to our history and providing me with a chance to learn about some important events in times past. In your lifetime I have connected to the legacy of brave women who became role models and mentors to me. Their work pushed me to learn, and to never be afraid to advocate for you.

Love,
Momma

A Gift of Gratitude

"We've got a responsibility to live up to the legacy of those who came before us by doing all that we can to help those who come after us."
Michelle Obama, Author

Gettysburg Leadership Institute

I never gave much thought to history. It was not a favorite subject of mine in school, even though we were forced to study it. For some reason, I just couldn't connect the dots that came from the past to the dots that were in my daily life or my future.

I'm so grateful to have had opportunities that led me to appreciate history a little more when Joe and I lived in Germany with our children. I have often said being there was like living in a fairy tale where castles peppered the mountain peaks. On sunny days it seemed their turrets could touch the clouds. Many were centuries old and had been homes to knights and the extraordinarily rich, yet that hadn't stopped the destruction caused by wars over the years.

What an incredible experience to walk on a cobblestone street that had been constructed by Romans in Trier, Germany. After exploring the World War II pillbox bunkers we found in France, that war was made real for me for the first time in my life. The pillboxes and bunkers were made from two-foot-thick concrete reinforced with steel rebar and then layered with a cast-iron armor covering. There were small look-out windows through which guns could be fired. It was eerie to look through those openings and imagine how the soldiers taking cover in them might have felt as they watched the enemy approach. Living in Europe changed my thoughts about history and the significance of events that happened before I lived.

That perspective is something I valued when I had an opportunity to spend a weekend with some young parent leaders from around the nation a few years ago. We traveled in buses from Washington, D.C. to Gettysburg, Pennsylvania, the site of major Civil War fighting. There, we had the chance to experience a condensed version of the Gettysburg Leadership Institute. More than 100 parent leaders and young adults with Down syndrome filled the training room. The facilitators tailored their presentation to leadership of the National Down Syndrome Society and local affiliates. They shared strategies from one of the Gettysburg battles, Pickett's Charge, and applied them to the role of advocates and the work we do. At the close of the event, we walked the battlefield and were given even more facts and strategies we could apply to our advocacy work. I was amazed that a battle that had occurred more than 150 years before could provide great lessons to our organization. Three important takeaways were:

1. **Meet your community's needs.** Organizations must be ready to provide support or resources when their community needs them.

2. **Drop the ego.** Staff and volunteers of organizations must always do what is right for the group, even if that means giving up the spotlight.

3. **Strategic vision is critical**. Without a vision for the future, a solid plan, there can be no effective path forward. It must be communicated to the entire organization and the community it serves.

As we waited to board the bus for our return to D.C. I overheard a conversation between three moms who had young children with Down syndrome. They obviously knew each other, based on their conversation. "We have to be strong advocates, you know. Parents before us never advocated as we do," I heard one of them say.

These were younger moms, and they hadn't yet learned all that had already happened in the disability community. I once was like them, uninformed about the work of the moms and dads years before Matt was born.

As a polite, older mom, I didn't intrude on their circle, but I have replayed that conversation many times in the years since. Had I been a bit pushier, I might have said, "You don't believe parents before you were strong advocates, the way you are? Let me tell you about the moms who came before you and those who even came before me. I know I'm an old mom in your eyes, but without the work I did, and many before me, you and your children would not have what you have today."

I would have helped them understand that it was parents like me who are the reason their little ones are in inclusive classrooms in their neighborhood schools. I would have helped them understand that what their babies, toddlers, and school-age kids experience today didn't exist in the fifties, sixties, and seventies. Years of advocacy, and pushing, and struggling made early intervention and educational inclusion happen. Additional advocacy work has opened opportunities for our young adults to participate in routine activities daily, like working and living in their community.

Even though it's cliché, I have always believed that history can repeat itself, so it's important we learn about what happened before us. There is no need, and frankly no time, for me to find a chisel and stone to create a wheel. Someone did that—I just need to build on that work to roll forward. If I had the platform, I would have helped those parents understand what their grandparents' and their great-grandparents' generations had done to create a world that is a little more accepting of their sweet children.

I have wondered if those young moms knew that there was a time when our babies would have been put to death. During World War II, Hitler had more than 300,000 physically and mentally disabled people killed because he deemed them "unworthy of living." I learned that it wasn't just the Jewish people who Hitler targeted and that my baby boy would have been part of that

group. History suddenly became terrifyingly real to me. In the United States, it was different, as a shortage of workers during the war led many companies to hire people with disabilities. Later, with the large number of veterans who had lost limbs in the war, physical disability was more evident and accepted. Even so, those with intellectual disability were often locked away in large institutions under the 1913 Mental Defectives Act.

As late as the mid-seventies, mothers who gave birth to babies with Down syndrome were encouraged to send them to large state-run institutions, go home, and forget about them. (Remember, I was one of those moms who got that speech from my own pediatrician.) Fortunately for all of us, there were moms in the fifties who said, "No, my baby deserves to live with his family. He will go home with me."

I didn't know it then, but they made my difficult path easier. I will be forever grateful to those moms who raised their children at home. They opened the doors that made it possible for Matt to live in and be loved by his family.

The Birth of Parent Organizations

The state of Minnesota played a big role in the changes we have seen in this country related to people with intellectual disabilities. More than seventy-five years ago, in the late forties, the American Association on Mental Deficiency (AAMD) supported a new movement created by parents. Some of the professionals in this group were concerned about the demands that parents had but also saw the opportunity to co-opt their numbers in lobbying for better institutions. Fortunately, the incoming president of the AAMD, Mildred Thomson, believed parents should have their own organizations. The National Association of Parents and Friends of the Mentally Retarded held their first conference in 1950 in Minneapolis. (I was two years old!)

There is strength in numbers, and moms began talking about the needs their children had for an education. In the 1950s and 1960s, when the public schools would not allow their children to attend classes, these parents started programs in the basements of neighborhood churches. But they didn't stop there.

In the sixties when some people were advocating for peace and free love while wearing flowers in their hair and smoking pot, there were parents who led grassroots efforts for more community-based programs for their children and for emotional support for their families. The tireless efforts of the families before me brought about laws that would change how people with disabilities were educated, how they lived, worked, and played. In the mid-1970s, new federal legislation—the Education of All Handicapped Children Act (now known as IDEA) was created. Finally, little ones could go to their neighborhood schools. However, some school districts decided that kids with disabilities would do better in segregated settings where they would have dedicated therapists and other specialists to provide for their unique needs. That was a beginning. Still, many began to see that segregated settings did not help children with disabilities be a part of their neighborhoods and communities. So, by the early nineties, families across the country were pushing for more inclusion of students with disabilities. They believed their children and the other students would both benefit from sharing classroom experiences.

There are still plenty of battles between families and schools, but we've made significant progress. I am grateful that families continue to push for what is right because not only are children given an opportunity to be educated along with their neighborhood peers, but some have formed lifelong friendships with their classmates. Some others are now experiencing life on college campuses. We've come a long way from the church basements, and all of us are better for that.

A Mother's Fight

In the early 1980s, an Iowa mom, Julie Beckett, fought the federal government to overturn a Medicaid rule that would have put her little girl, Katie, in a nursing home for care. At that time, Katie had medical needs that were covered by Medicaid, but payment could only be made to a hospital or nursing home. Julie argued that if the nursing services and necessary medical equipment were provided in their home, Katie could live with her family and the government would save money. Julie won the battle, and the Katie Beckett Waiver has since served more than a half-million children with significant healthcare needs who would have otherwise not been able to live in their family home. Families touched by Julie's advocacy are grateful.

A person who qualifies for Medicaid (income-based) has a right to medical services provided in institutional settings. When a person uses a Medicaid Waiver they "waive the right to institutional care." Through waivers like a Home and Community Based Services (HCBS) waiver, people receive the needed services in their community.

Taking on the IRS

In 2014, the advocacy of parents led to monumental legislation that amended the IRS Code to create tax-free savings accounts for individuals with disabilities. Learning about that legislation a few years after it had passed, I could hardly believe what I had heard. Shortly after Matt left school in 1996, he entered a time in his life when there was no funding for adult services in Florida. Joe and I paid privately for Matt to attend a center-based activity one day a week so he could have something to do. It was then I wondered why we couldn't have set up the special savings accounts many families establish to help fund college educations. My thought was that those funds could help pay for some services once their kids entered the adult world. That's as far as my idea ever got. It never left my head, mostly because I didn't know what to do with it.

I am a firm believer that there are no coincidences. I still get goosebumps when I think of the "Godwink" I've received related to that crazy idea that went nowhere. You see in 2005—nearly ten years later—Stephen Beck, Jr. sat at his kitchen table in Northern Virginia and worried about the future for his daughter with Down syndrome. He spoke with other parents about the stress he felt because he couldn't save for his daughter like he could for his other child. As he talked with those parents about his worry, it so happened that one of them lived next door to the Chief of Staff for Representative Ander Crenshaw of Florida. After hearing from the parents, Representative Crenshaw started the long and grueling process to introduce and pass legislation. It took nine years of hard work and education of members of Congress, but these parents, joined by many others, never let go of their dream. The result was the Achieving a Better Life Experience (ABLE) Act. This was a fully bipartisan effort and had the support of 85%

of the US Congress—how wonderful was that? The ABLE Act allows families to save money in a tax-free account that can be used by the person with a disability for education, transportation, housing, or other qualified disability expenses. As I write, nearly 65,000 people (Matt being one of them) have opened ABLE accounts. I am grateful that this idea grew from a thought to legislation that is helping Matt and so many others.

So, in 2017, when I heard about the ABLE Act, I felt a twinge of embarrassment—that I had done nothing with the idea when it came to me. Of course, I recall that I had been busy parenting a young adult with Down syndrome and hadn't yet made a connection between my life and political advocacy. With that momentary sense of shame came a surge of excitement knowing that my never-shared thought had come to another parent who did do something about it. And now children and adults with disabilities can have savings accounts that do not interfere with their access to other government benefits. It was then I realized that we need to share our ideas—our dreams—no matter how unusual they may seem. Advocacy ideas, goals, and dreams all need to be given a voice. You never know where it might lead.

And here is the "Godwink" moment (there are no coincidences) that I mentioned earlier. In the Spring of 2019, a small room in the United States Capitol was filled with children and adults with Down syndrome, their parents, and other advocates. It was there that I received a National Down Syndrome Society (NDSS) Champion of Change award presented annually to an advocate who has contributed significantly to the Down syndrome community. The award I received was named for someone who had been a tireless advocate and had been the Vice Chairman of the Board of NDSS prior to his passing in 2014. I still get a lump in my throat, and I am filled with joy, when I recognize the significance of this award—the Stephen Beck, Jr. Award—for the father who carried through on the idea that I had so many years before and championed the ABLE Act.

As I think through the four decades of Matt's life, I feel a strong sense of gratitude to the trailblazing moms (and dads) from the forties, fifties, and sixties. Matt and I, and all of us, are benefitting from

Kandi Pickard, President, and CEO of the National Down Syndrome Society presented me with the Stephen Beck, Jr. Champion of Change Award in the Spring of 2019. Washington, D.C.

progress over the years—from a single-lane dirt path to a paved road to a multi-lane superhighway.

Enjoy the ride, mothers, and fathers of today, but do take time to:

- Check out the historical markers along your journey.

- Give thanks to moms and dads who wouldn't accept no for an answer.

- Share your ideas, your dreams—no matter how unusual they may seem

My Gift to You

Appreciation and gratitude come from knowing our history. We have been fortunate and have been given many gifts in the last seventy-five years because there were parents who felt their children deserved better lives. We have a rich history of parents making changes for children and adults with Down syndrome and other disabilities. In Matt's lifetime there have been significant changes in how we raise, how we educate, and how we support people with disabilities. I think the stories of the Katie Beckett Waiver and the ABLE Act are great examples of the importance of parent advocacy. I have learned that no idea is crazy and those ideas that pop in my head need to be voiced so they can gather energy from others. I encourage every parent, every sibling, every person who cares about a person with Down syndrome or other type of disability, to act on their ideas. You never know when you just might change the world.

1. What surprised you the most about the work that has been done by parents for children with disabiities?

_____

_____

_____

2. Knowing the role that parents played in making changes, what do you feel the most gratitude for?

_____

_____

_____

3. Based on past parent advocacy successes, in what area will you build your advocacy skills?

_____

_____

_____

A GIFT OF HOPE

Dear Matt,

I have given a lot of thought to what I was going to say in this letter to you. As I have traveled through time to reflect on our life together, this gift has been the most difficult one to write about. Thinking back on the years you were in school has brought me to tears and has resurfaced doubts that I thought I had let go of long ago.

I guess this letter is one that is not only of thanks but also a letter of apology. I want you to know that I saw your pain, and I was powerless to find a way to help you through it. I know now that I made a lot of mistakes during those years, but they were not made because I didn't care—they happened because I just didn't know what to do. I am sorry, Matt, that it took me, and all those who were supporting you, so awfully long to figure it all out.

My thanks to you is for helping me have hope. I now know that it is hope that carried me through those difficult years. I always had hope that the next day would be better, that the next doctor would have an answer, that somehow, I could help you smile again. Hope gave me a sense of resilience—something I needed to stay strong enough to do what was necessary to support you. I have come to realize that your gift of hope has helped me through many difficult periods of my life. When I have hope, I am in a space where I find optimism and energy. Those are two key elements that drive me and help me create whatever is needed for success.

And so, Matt, I thank you for showing me that hope can keep us moving forward when everything around us seems to be crashing down.

Love,
Momma

A Gift of Hope

"Hope is the thing with feathers that perches in the soul and sings the tune without the words and never stops."

Emily Dickinson, Poet

As I have closely examined my life with Matt, I recognize how often I found that I survived only because I had hope. In fact, there were many times that hope fueled my optimism, gave me energy, and filled me with strength. I recently watched *The Christmas Train*, a movie adapted from a book of the same name, written by David Baldacci. One line caught my ear, and it touched my heart as it so clearly defined what hope was for me. "Hope begins when you stand in the dark looking out at the light." Often, in the most troubling times, I felt I was in darkness—it was when I found something to hope for that the light began to shine again for me.

In no part of Matt's life did I need hope to continue to support him and give him the life he deserved, as much as I did in the period around which this chapter is written. This has been the most difficult part of the book to write, and I believe you will understand as you read.

Brought to My Knees

During our time in Germany, I was just about brought to my knees. Matt had begun showing signs of aggression in school during the spring of 1982, just before our move. His teacher wrote on a few occasions of him pulling on the clothing of others, but it appears from the school communication book that there was no intervention taken.

Joe was an Army Warrant Officer, assigned to the Criminal Investigation Division (think detective), and was also trained in protective services to accompany the Secretary of Defense or other high-level military leaders on trips abroad. Shortly after we arrived in Germany, he was sent on a protective service mission out of the country for ten days. That left me alone with the boys in a new country I didn't yet know.

Our apartment was nice, a former high-ranking officers' quarters after World War II. Although we were on the third floor, I soon adjusted to the stairwell living, as it was known. (We were one of eight families sharing our four-story stairwell.) Opening the only door in and out of our apartment took us to a hallway with the bathroom to the left (it was spacious, and that I loved). The

boys' bedrooms were on the right side of that hallway, with Matt's room closer to the entry door and Michael's farther down the hall. The door to Joe's and my bedroom was straight ahead as I entered the apartment. Our bedroom was roomy, even with the closets that appeared to have been added in later. There was also a small, built-in dressing table with a mirror, which I found to be practical and fun. Back in the hallway and just beyond the bathroom door was another door that led into an unusually shaped kitchen. A small galley with lots of storage space, both overhead and below the countertop, was just inside that kitchen doorway. That area provided me plenty of room for the pottery collection I built while we lived there. At the end of the counter was the refrigerator—the great keeper of wonderful German delights like pastries, wursts, breads and, of course, wine and beer. Just past the refrigerator was another doorway to the living room. On the other side of that door was a built-in banquette. This is where the kitchen made an L-shaped turn; across from the banquette was my stove and sink, along with a little more storage and countertop. Windows next to the banquette provided plenty of light and a pretty view of the green belt between our quarters and the military housing behind us. Back out that second kitchen door in the corner was another small dining area and the large living room. Windows that opened outward covered most of the south wall in the living room, as well, so there was always lots of natural light coming in.

Just before we arrived in the country, the military housing section had removed safety rails from the windows in all the military quarters. And because there were no mosquitoes and flies, there were no screens on the windows, either. We used household furnishings from the government while we waited for our personal belongings to arrive. The sofa we were using had removable cushions that Matt loved to pull off and scatter around the floor.

Matt loved looking out the windows in our living room in Germany. That smile and laughter were not often seen or heard shortly after this photo was taken. Fall 1982, Vogelweh, Germany

While Joe was away on that first mission, Matt figured out that he could stack those cushions by the open window so he could watch the kids playing in that green space behind our quarters. Fortunately, I came into the living room just as he had finished stacking three cushions and had climbed on them. Apparently, he still couldn't see the kids, so he jumped just enough to propel himself to the window's edge. I reached him at the very moment his head and chest flew out the window, grabbed one of his ankles and pulled him back inside. I still get a sick feeling thinking about what might have happened had I not been close enough to get to him before he launched himself out and down three flights to the ground below. Life with Matt was getting more challenging, and I hoped I could at least keep him safe as I took steps to get the rails put back on our windows.

Hope to Understand

Life got harder for all of us as Matt became more difficult to interact with. About a year after we had arrived in Germany, he lost interest in many of his toys and cooperated less and less. Still not toilet trained when he was eight years old, at bedtime he wore the largest disposable diapers I could find. Usually, it

160

wasn't an issue, but one morning as I was about to wake him for school, the odor of a dirty diaper met me in the hallway outside his room. As I opened the door and entered his bedroom, I exclaimed, "What have you done, Matt? Just look at this mess!"

I was in tears as I led him to the bathroom for a quick scrub-down. Needless, to say I was happy to put him on the school bus that morning. My legs were heavy as I trudged back up the three flights of stairs where the dirty diaper waited for me. I got a pan of hot, soapy water, an old cloth, a scrub brush, and some rubber gloves, ready to enter the hazard field that was Matt's bedroom. During the night, he had ripped off his dirty diaper. And since he was awake, he decided to finger paint his sheets, his bed, and the wall next to it. As I cleaned, I hoped Matt would soon be toilet trained.

A few months after the diaper incident, just before Matt fell asleep, we heard glass shatter. He had been in his room for about half an hour, making noises and doing whatever he could to stay awake. Joe and I ran to his room to find him sitting cross-legged on his bed and grinning. Laying on the wide windowsill was his favorite teddy bear, covered in shards of glass. The glass had sprayed across the room and made it unsafe to enter barefoot. Since Joe still had his shoes on, he went in and sat on the bed with Matt while I went for my shoes and the broom. Although I had glass to clean up, I was grateful that the housing office had agreed, months earlier, to put those safety rails back on our windows for Matt's protection. Sweeping up the glass, my hope was that I would, one day, be able to understand my little boy.

Photographs and Memories

Life in our home became even more challenging as time went on. Matt was unhappy and becoming unreachable. If you recall, Matt had not yet been diagnosed as Autistic or with Apraxia and I thought I was simply raising a difficult child with Down syndrome. I felt inadequate as a mom and as his advocate. The roller coaster we had been stuck on seemed to run out of control for years.

Nearing the completion of writing this book, I decided to review old records, letters, and pictures of Matt that I have kept in an army trunk in our garage. In this trunk, I found a treasure chest filled with papers and snapshots, but I also found some extremely difficult reading in the school communication books. Each entry brought increased pain as I relived the days that I had somewhat successfully buried in my memory bank.

Page after page of the notebooks from our time in Germany were filled with written documentation of the struggles Matt had every day in those years, and as a result, each of us who loved him shared those struggles. Reading once more of the hitting, the screaming, the pinching, kicking and loud outbursts, my heart literally ached, even though nearly forty years had passed. It took me several days to get through those journals and pictures because the tears flowed freely and without control. At times, sobs crept out as I wrestled with a sense of failure once again.

Days after I had delved into the layers of those difficult years, I recognized the gift of hope that was hidden in the anguish during those days of chaos.

I was surprised at the number of photos I found in that old trunk in the garage. Even with the calendar telling me it was December, the above-average temperatures in Florida made it uncomfortable to stay long in the warm, humid garage. I gathered a large armful of pictures and some of the notebooks and returned to the comfort of my air-conditioned living room. I sat in my small white rattan rocker and placed part of the stack of mementos on the table next to me. I placed some in my lap and others fell onto the cool marble tiled floor where they stayed for a while. Transported through time, I easily remembered the details of each of those photos.

Sorting through them, I picked up a photo that age had faded somewhat. In this picture, we are sitting on the sofa of our first home—behind me, the window is covered by the daisy-splashed orange, green, yellow, and gold draperies my grandmother, Echo, had helped me sew three years earlier. Michael is sitting beside me, and I

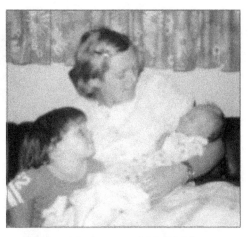

Michael, Jadene, and Matt at home shortly after his birth. August 1974, Melbourne, Florida

am holding Matt securely in my left arm. He is tiny, just three or four days old. My smile hides the pain of the reality that is about to change our lives forever. I am looking at Matt, only wanting to protect him and help him grow healthy and strong. The features that characterize the diagnosis are quite evident to me these forty-eight years later—extremely small, low-set ears, the flat bridge on his button nose, the slant of his eyes and the tiny curve on his littlest fingers. I'm glad I wasn't aware of all that was ahead of us on this journey. I might have been afraid to breathe—something like I was feeling in those days as I sorted through the photos and papers.

Two black and white photos had also fallen onto my lap. They were probably taken within a few minutes of each other. In the first one, Matt, who was then two months old, is lying on his stomach with his head lifted off the floor. In the other photo he is lying on his back with his head turned toward Michael. They

Michael and Matt on the quilt made by my Aunt Virginia. September 1974, Melbourne, Florida

are both on the blue and white satin quilt my Aunt Virginia had sewn for Matt. Michael has a huge smile on his face, perhaps because he has already decided to confiscate his brother's quilt— trading it for the one that she had knitted for him. That quilt became Michael's "cold blankie," and he cherished it for many years, until it was in shreds.

The rest of the photos were scattered around the floor, and I spied one of my most favorite of Matt. It was snapped in 1976 at the time that Joe was about to leave to re-enlist in the army; he wanted some pictures of the boys to keep with him while he was away at training. Approximately two-and-a-half years old, Matt is sitting on the ground in a park where we had taken the boys. He is tickled and has an adorable expression on

Matt enjoying the park in Melbourne, Florida. Fall 1976

his face that has always warmed my heart whenever I looked at that picture.

Other photos include a happy little boy riding on his hobby horse, and one where he is chasing the pigeons in the walkplatz in Kaiserslautern, Germany; he seemed to be happiest when he was in motion. One of the last pictures I discovered was more recent, taken outside our home in Clearwater. He is helping Joe lay brick along the edge of the driveway and from the look on his face, he was taking his job quite seriously.

Matt riding the hobby horse he got from Santa.
December 1982, Vogelweh, Germany

Matt chasing pigeons, with Doug Mantooth
keeping up. Fall 1983, Kaiserslautern, Germany

Matt helping his dad lay brick along the edge of the
driveway at our home. Clearwater, Florida

Hope Carried Me Through

There were more pictures deep in the bottom of the trunk—
several of the Heim mit Sonderschule, the German residential
school Matt was sent to during the last year we were stationed
there. Although not an experience I would have chosen for Matt
or our family, it gave us the time we all needed to regroup and
time to hope that we could once again find our way.

For days, I sorted through piles of pictures and notebooks.
Messages written by me or Joe to whatever teacher Matt had
in his life at the time were filled with daily reminders of the
problems he was developing.

Almost a half dozen notebooks from the school years
between the fall of 1982 through February 1985 were filled

Another photo of the residential school Matt attended while we were in Germany. Heim mit Sonderschule, Herxheim, Germany

with glimpses into Matt's days. As I read through them, the pattern of difficult behaviors increased each year. I believe that while I was living that life, the impact of his behaviors was overwhelming, and I did whatever I could to get from one day to the next. Looking back, I can see the strength and hope I had to have—that Joe and Michael also had to have—or we may not have endured.

In Germany, I volunteered at the Army Community Service (ACS) center for our local military community. Every ACS center was mandated to have an Exceptional Family Member Program. Most centers in Europe met the Department of Defense minimum requirement to have resource information on services for family members with disabilities at every U.S. Army post worldwide.

My experience as a parent and a certified teacher told me right
away that there was a need for more than file drawers filled
with papers. As a volunteer, I expanded the program to include
parent support, and the continuation of the summer camp that
had begun in 1981, the year before our arrival. I worked in
partnership with a Department of Defense Dependent Schools
(DoDDS) teacher, Bruce Steffensmier, who had been involved
with Special Olympics International prior to coming to Germany.
Together we formed a committee that provided opportunities
for students with disabilities to participate in basketball, baseball,
bowling, and other sports. We eventually hosted a combined
German American Special Olympics event which was well-
received in both the military and the German communities.
With Doug Mantooth, our friend and Matt's teacher, I helped
establish a work program for the teens in the special education
class. We coordinated with a German sheltered workshop and
brought piecework to the ACS center for the teens to do one day
a week. One other day, some of the students went to paid jobs
in our military community. For the first time since I left Iowa,
I felt a strong sense of belonging. I could see that my work was
important to me and to others.

Some days it was tough to balance Matt's needs with my own
needs and those of the rest of the family. As days turned to
months and then to years, it became even more difficult. The
time and energy it took to be a wife, a mom, and an employee
was exhausting. At the end of each day, I was faced with
messages from Matt's teacher that were so similar, it was almost
unnecessary to read them.

Here is a sample of what came home from his teacher day after
day in 1984:

August 27: "We saw lots of kicking and some hitting and yelling. He also pulled a drawer out, tipped tables and kicked chairs."

August 28: "Lots of kicking, hitting, and some yelling today. We can't leave Matt alone."

September 26: "A very difficult morning, loud, aggressive all day."

Imagine reading notes similar to these for such a long time. Matt did have some good days, but they were rare. It seemed to me that the school personnel were more focused on what Matt was doing wrong, and they didn't comment on anything but the problems. Matt was troubled and no one uncovered the reason why.

That disruptive classroom behavior led to a request for behavioral support services, as well as a consultation and following by a child psychiatrist. Matt was referred to Occupational and Physical Therapists (OT and PT). None of them had any answers. The DoDDS Behavior Management Specialist and his teachers attempted to address the behaviors that occurred regularly— hitting and kicking others and objects, throwing anything within reach, knocking down dividers, chairs, waste baskets, and desks, tearing up materials (books, papers, posters, displays), pulling down curtains, pulling at clothing (his and others), pulling hair, and yanking on jewelry, pinching, biting, blowing mucous, and making loud noises. Unsuccessful approaches included the use of a time-out room, use of a time-out chair, time out restrained on the floor, and an ammonia capsule as an aversive stimulus. Regardless of these efforts, Matt's behavior did not improve. (I had not yet learned that behavior is communication and I do not know if the professionals knew that in the mid-eighties. Regardless, Matt's communication was never addressed—the focus stayed on the "bad" behaviors.)

The report following his OT eval stated, "Matt was uncooperative and aggressive toward the examiner. He pulled at the examiner's sweater and necklace. It appeared that this was a deliberate, planned behavior. Sensory accommodation is generally dysfunctional, and Matt becomes easily over stimulated which frequently results in aggressive behavior."

When the DoDDS personnel announced that they didn't believe they could handle Matt, I insisted that they had an obligation to provide him an appropriate education. I showed them the Department of Defense Directive, and they decided it would be acceptable to teach him in a makeshift classroom—on the stage, behind the curtain in the auditorium. A teacher was hired to work with him one-on-one, and he could attend school for only half a day. It wasn't surprising that Matt found it distracting when the auditorium was used as a gym for P.E. classes. There were days that he cried all morning, days that he turned his desk and chair over, or threw the counting blocks across the room.

Music always soothed Matt, and I love that even today, with my voice terribly off-key, he finds a place of serenity when I sing. In hope that I could find some comfort for my troubled little boy, I taught the teacher his favorite songs – *White Coral Bells*, *Kumbaya*, and *Itsy-Bitsy Spider.* Unfortunately, at that point in time, nothing seemed to soothe him.

We attended many meetings to review the latest behaviors, the strategies that had been implemented and failed, and possible next steps. Despite everything attempted to assist Matt with behavior control, he grew more unpredictable. When that little classroom didn't seem to work, the DoDDS personnel decided they would no longer serve Matt, and directed us to place him in a residential program back in the States. Their claim was that they had no further responsibility for Matt's education. Once again, I cited the DOD Directive and stated that their inability to serve Matt would impact Joe's assignment and would be a career-ender for him.

It Wasn't Enough

My heart hurt because I could not find a way to help my child. I had gathered strength I didn't know I had and fought as hard as I could for his rights to an education, but it wasn't enough.

This was one of the saddest times in my life. I felt like I had failed Matt again. Even as my heart broke, I knew that he had rights that the school was trampling. The DoDDS system gave us information on Devereux in Pennsylvania and the Brown School in Texas. Reluctantly, I completed the application for Devereux. Later, the DoDDS area representative, Dr. Fred Killian, called me and said, "Mrs. Ransdell, you haven't filled out this form correctly. You should have indicated that you and Mr. Ransdell will be responsible for payment on this placement."

Seriously? I thought. My heart started pounding. I could feel the blood rush to my face as I gathered all the strength I had gained in the years since Matt was born. As calmly and politely as I could, I replied, "I'm sorry, Dr. Killian, but you are wrong. I have completed the application correctly. It is not our choice to send our child back to the States. The DoDDS system is responsible for providing Matt a free and appropriate education, and it is DoDDS who must pay for him to attend another school."

There was an uncomfortable silence for a moment before Dr. Killian replied, "Well, Mrs. Ransdell, you have not explored all

the options here in Germany and that must be done before we proceed with a stateside placement."

"Once again," I began, "it was your office who told me there were no schools here in Germany that would serve a child who has behavior difficulties and an intellectual disability. I was informed that the German schools serve children with one or the other but not both. If you know of a program that hasn't been ruled out, please let me know."

"I have to go right now," Dr. Killian said. "But there is another school that I think would welcome Matt. It's a residential program in Herxheim run by the Catholic Church. I am meeting with the principal later today and will ask about the possibility of Matt attending."

After I hung up the phone, my hands were sweating, and my stomach was in knots. I was just learning to be assertive with people in authority and it made me uncomfortable. I did, however, give myself a little pat on the back for having the strength to stand up for Matt. At that moment, even with the physical signs of nervousness, I had hope that I could make life just a bit better for Matt as I was learning to advocate for his rights.

Chickens Swimming in the Pond

Dr. Killian called me a few days later and said he had held a productive conversation with the principal and that we had been invited to visit the school and the residences. Within a couple of weeks, Dr. Killian and the DoDDS Special Education Specialist drove Joe, Matt, and me to Herxheim where we met with the principal, toured the school, and visited the residential cottages. Because the school was more than forty-five minutes from us, Matt would need to live there if he were accepted. Late the next week, I got another call from Dr. Killian who was quite pleased to tell me that the Heim mit Sonderschule had agreed that Matt could attend. They felt they could help this little boy of mine that others could not reach.

I hated that he would no longer live with us but was glad that I had remained strong. It meant that Joe was able to finish his assignment, our family could stay in Germany, and that Matt was close enough to visit us every other weekend. The people who worked at the school and cared for Matt in his little home quickly grew to love him. It was at Herxheim that Matt was seen as a child, not just as a problem to be dealt with. I began to have hope for Matt's future once again. Matt learned to smile again. My heart smiled, too!

Matt attended the Heim mit Sonderschule in Herxheim during the last eleven months of Joe's assignment in Germany. Although this was a Catholic-run school and residence, most of the staff were civilians from the Herxheim area. I don't recall ever seeing nuns or a priest, although, logic tells me they were most likely a part of the program. We could have no contact with him for at least the first two months, and when the school personnel felt he was ready, they would transport him every other weekend for home visits. I thought, at the time, that I wouldn't be able to function without seeing Matt for so long. My heart was heavy because I was not the one who kissed my little boy goodnight, but I also had hope that life would change for Matt at his new school. Fortunately, I had my volunteer work to do and that helped the time pass.

We learned that Matt had adjusted quite well, and he got his first weekend visit just six weeks after he had left us. When he came home, he smiled and laughed. I cried when I saw that smile on his sweet face, once again. We received several letters from the principal within a couple of months of Matt's enrollment. In every letter, written in German and translated for us by one of Joe's German civilian office support staff, the principal wrote such nice things about Matt. He did not fill those communications with all the problems that Matt was having, but shared stories of the cute things that Matt was doing.

If you recall, we had chosen to use total communication (a combination of spoken words paired with signs) with Matt. He had a small spoken vocabulary and used some signs, but he was never consistent with either, and that often led to frustration for all of us when we didn't understand him.

In one letter to us, the principal wrote of the house parents in Matt's cottage spending time with him at a little pond on the school property. There were ducks in the pond and Matt loved to watch them swim. He would use the sign for chicken when he saw the ducks, so the story in that letter was about Matt watching the chickens swimming in the pond. I always felt good when I read those letters because I knew that my baby was loved and cared for. Even then, in the midst of it all, I started to feel that my hope for the future was realistic.

We had a meeting with the administration in Herxheim just before Michael and I returned to the States. (Joe and Matt stayed in Germany for about six more weeks, as I had hoped to get services in place for Matt by the time he arrived in Florida.) The school principal told me they loved having Matt there. They had never worked with an American student before and found him to be a delight. He suggested that since Matt was doing so well, we could leave him in Herxheim, and he would personally fly to the States on holidays so Matt could visit us. Of course, we couldn't agree to that arrangement!

What Had Changed?

I have given a lot of thought to what changed for Matt when he was in Herxheim. I sorted through all the pieces and came away with several conditions that changed between the DoDDS classroom and the residential school.

There seemed to be two major differences. First, the school and residential staff did not treat disruptive behavior with medications, and they asked our permission to eliminate them. At first, we were reluctant but placed our trust in these caring people. Within a few months, he was free of the psychiatric medications that the military doctor had prescribed.

The second difference, I believe, was the attitude of the people working with Matt. I always felt that the teacher primarily responsible for Matt his last year in the DoDDS school defined him by his behaviors, forgetting or ignoring he was also a little boy. On more than one occasion, Doug shared with me things the other teacher had said or done that indicated she did not want to deal with a student who wasn't compliant.

When Matt went to Herxheim, he was greeted by people who saw a cute, blonde-hair, blue-eyed little boy. They saw he had difficulty interacting with others, but instead of yelling at him or scolding him, they gave him many hugs and lots of kindness. It was obvious that the extra care made a huge difference in

Matt's willingness to participate and interact more appropriately. I believe the compassion of the staff at Herxheim was felt by Matt. I think he knew that people finally saw him and heard him. And it was then that I allowed myself to hope that his separation from us was making a difference and that one day we would have a happy child again.

Matt lived and went to school in Herxheim for eleven months. And what an amazing transformation occurred for him. When Matt came back to us, he still had difficulties, but we could communicate with him and help him when he got upset. We had hope, once again, that Matt could be reached with the right supports and that he would find his way.

As I look back now, having reflected on the pain of those years (and a few after our return to the States), I can see how hope is what carried me through those extremely difficult times.

- Hope gave me a sense of resilience to find optimism and energy.

- Hope kept me going when positive outcomes seemed unreachable.

- Hope was the lifeline that I clung to until Matt found his way back to us.

My Gift to You

A gift of hope. What a wonderful thing to receive. Hope can help us make the hard parts of our lives more tolerable. Hope can be the thing that encourages us to keep moving and take the steps we need to reach a better outcome. And hope can buy us time to create solutions to some of life's most difficult periods.

1. Think of a situation in your life in which you needed to hold on to hope. Write about it below.

_____

_____

_____

2. How did having hope help you to focus on a solution or better outcome?

_____

_____

_____

3. If hope fades, what can you do to bring it back?

_____

_____

_____

4. What gives you hope in your life?

_____

_____

_____

5. Think about a person you know who has a disability challenge. What do you think is their biggest hope?

_____

_____

_____

A GIFT OF LETTING GO

Dear Matt,

I'm here, once again, to say thank you. Reflecting on our life together has led me to understand how deeply fortunate I have been. I have learned to look at life with a sense of gratitude for the opportunities I have been given, and that has helped me handle some difficult periods. There have been times when I struggled with what was happening in our life, responding with anger, fear, and sadness. Yet, I watched you live your life as an adult with a quiet resolve. What an inspiration you have been, and still are!

This last gift of letting go is one that I am still holding close. Through the process of letting go, I have watched you take life in stride when those around you react to the latest life situation. It doesn't matter to you if you have pizza on Thanksgiving because your staff doesn't know how to cook. In my head, that's just wrong and you have been slighted. I spend time fretting, and you enjoy every bite of your favorite food. When the pandemic hit, I worried about your health, who you were coming in contact with, and if you would ever be able to go back to the Veterans Administration volunteer job you loved. You have been content to be at home, watch your favorite movies, play with your sticks, and go on occasional car rides. You are able to let go of the trivial things that don't really matter.

You and Michael have both taught me that letting go is part of our lives. I originally experienced it when you were born and I let go of the dreams I had for you—first, that you would be a girl, and then new dreams I created for your life before I was aware that you had Down syndrome. I learned to let go when you were a teenager and I realized I would never hear you say, "I love you." I had to let go when your brother went off to see the world in the Coast Guard, got married, and had children. It was hard watching him leave home and no longer need me as he did when he was a child.

And I had to let go again when you gave me a thumb up after I asked if you wanted to be like Mike and live in your own home, away from your mom and dad. Just as with Michael, it was hard to let you go but you have found a life that is perfect for you. You showed me that, even though your life didn't look exactly like Michael's, it was still quite good. As a volunteer in the VA hospital you showed me that you are happy in your life. Letting the doors close that, in some ways, held you back, gave us the chance to see you grow into the man you are today.

More recently, I have learned to let go of my perception of how I should be a support to you. And I've had to let go of my youth and embrace the reality of the years passing by and our aging. There have been some difficult moments in these most recent times of letting go.

I'm so glad that throughout your life you have been teaching me that letting go does not have to be a bad experience. You and Michael have also shown me that letting go does not mean quitting or giving up. I've learned that as life changes, new opportunities arise. To be ready for those new beginnings, I have had to close some doors so that others can open. It wasn't always easy, but it has been worth the effort.

These times of letting go have helped me appreciate all that I have had in my life. So now I thank both you and Michael for helping me cherish what was, and to be open to what comes next.

Love,
Momma

A Gift of Letting Go

*"Sometimes letting things go is
an act of far greater power than
defending or hanging on."*

Eckhart Tolle,
Author and Spiritual Leader

It's hard to imagine that the birth of a child with a disability
would teach me about letting go. One would think that
such a pivotal experience would have had me holding on
for dear life. But the truth is that letting go has been a part of
the journey from the beginning.

Letting go has a daunting connotation, I suppose. It can indicate
the end of many things; but the beauty of letting go is that it can
also signal the start of something new. I have experienced many
periods of letting go through Matt's life; I've let go of dreams,
of people, of expectations, and even responsibilities. Some of

185

those times I've let go were painful—the death of my husband being one of the most difficult. Yet I have found comfort in other times of letting go. Knowing Matt has someone who is watching out for him, taking on a responsibility I had for many years, has brought me peace as I move forward in my life.

Letting Go of Dreams of the Future

My first letting go was of dreams of the future. Matt was my second child, and we had hoped for a girl. Suddenly, I had to relinquish those visions of a son and daughter. And when we found Matt had Down syndrome, there went the thoughts I had of two boys who would grow up similarly. Letting go of the dream of a little girl was not difficult. It falls in the realm of adjusting and moving on without giving it much thought. At the time I shifted from dreams of a daughter to dreams of another son, I was still blissfully unaware of what was to come, and I was able to envision two little boys in my life. That dream held for just a day or two.

After his diagnosis, it took me some time to learn how to let go of that crushing reality. I had little understanding of what life could be for him. I had to let go of those dreams of two brothers growing up together. I didn't know what to do beyond that. But, one afternoon, when Matt was about six months old, I walked into his room as he was sleeping in his crib. It was the first time I was able to look at Matt and see him—my baby boy—and not his diagnosis. In that moment I let go of dreams that couldn't become realities. And from that moment forward, I was able to begin to dream new dreams for him. I had freed myself to develop some wonderful plans for Matt's future, and for my own. My ability to let go and reframe the future changed how I experienced each day and the way I moved through my life.

Life From His Window on the World

When Matt was a child and later a teenager, it became clear to me that he was on a different path than other young ones with Down syndrome. It was difficult for me because I couldn't figure out what I was doing wrong. I had plenty of people tell me I needed to do more, that I hadn't set my expectations high enough, and that I didn't place enough demands on Matt. Years passed and I was certain that, even with my training in exceptional education, I wasn't doing it right. I couldn't get Matt to talk to me; I couldn't teach him to read or write his name; I couldn't get him to participate fully in family activities. There were years I lived in the shadow of what could be, what should be. And then Matt grew up and he got out of the box everyone had put him in. (In public school, expecations for what Matt could do were kept low. He did not do well on standarized IQ tests and other assessments and was placed in the profoundly mentally handicapped classes.) He left the public school program that was supposed to be individualized, based on his skills and needs, but was really a canned program for groups of children with similar intellectual abilities.

Things began to change for Matt as we addressed his life from his window on the world. I was able to let go of the low expectations for him and let him blossom. We had been told that he would need to go to a day program where there was too much noise and not enough structure for him. So after public school, we focused on Matt—what he could do and what he enjoyed. We built on his strengths and and let him help us define his day. I'm pleased to say that when I moved out of his way, he grew into the most magnificent being who has led a life of his choosing and has touched the hearts of many.

Release of Guilt and Anger

Recently, I have allowed myself to focus more on my needs. I have slowly learned that I have permission to care for myself. The freedom I have found in letting go of my guilty conscience when I take time for myself has brought me comfort and a sense of peace. I have been exploring some feelings that have not served me well thoughout my life—those feelings of insecurity, feelings of unworthiness, and feelings of failure. They were hidden aspects of my life, yet they often influenced my actions. Finding strength and letting go of those pieces of me have helped me realize I don't have to prove anything to anyone.

Not long ago I had an "aha moment" that resulted in the release of guilt and anger I carried for most of Matt's life. I finally made a connection between three major events in my life. There was the guidance given to me by the Mailman Center professionals: "You must do more for Matt."; the condemnation of my girlfriends: "You spend too much time with Matt."; and the consideration that Joe had: "You need to spend more time with Michael and me." Those statements kept me in a constant state of anxiety. How could I have (all at the same time) not done enough and also have done too much and still need to do more? Knowing that if the balance wasn't just right my marriage could fail made me question everything I did.

Writing has helped me to identify the moments in my life where we strayed from the path just a bit. I recognized that my role as a parent to Matt was always quite different from Joe's role. And I suppose for many families, those roles are not the same. I know now that how much we loved our child was not determined by the level of involvement we had in Matt's life. I recall when I felt abandoned and a little angry the day Joe said, "You have

the degree in special education, so it's up to you—you know what's best for Matt."

I watched as he pulled back more and more in the decision-making, until all he did was rubber-stamp whatever I suggested we do. To me it felt he was uninvolved or uninterested. Rarely did he take the lead on something about Matt's life. I spent a number of years being angry about his passive involvement, but I was recently able to acknowledge that his support was enough. I recognized that my training made me more prepared to do the work as an advocate with the school systems, and later with the developmental disabilities program. It felt good letting go of my anger as I accepted that I had inadvertently pushed Joe out, and he willingly stepped aside because he trusted me. How I wished that I had understood this before his death.

It hasn't been easy admitting that I have sometimes created my own burdens, but once I understood that, I was in a place to no longer take it personally. Letting go of feeling hurt releases the anger, the resentment, and the other feelings that had limited my power. What a gift it has been to allow myself to own my feelings and actions.

Growing Older Together

We have all been growing older together. For the past few months, I have been much more aware of my age and my own mortality. I am living alone now, having lost my dear husband, Joe, to complications of COVID. Letting go of Joe has brought me to a door that I've been reluctant to go through. I find I am reflecting on all I have learned and all I have gathered from these gifts Matt has bestowed on me.

I don't get to see my son Michael as often as I would like as he now lives about seventy-five miles from me. He is working hard trying to establish a new manufacturing business in the slow economy of the current pandemic. I'm so proud of all he does to make it successful, just as I am proud of the love he showers on his boys. Michael, as a single father, is raising my two grandsons to be respectful young men.

Matt, of course, moved out of our home when he was in his early twenties. However, I have remained closely involved in his life and in his care. This season of aging brings two more opportunities for letting go. When I began writing this story, I had been told by Matt's neurologist that Matt had Alzheimer's disease and I was afraid that I would very soon be letting go of him one last time. Fortunately, he has not shown progression of the disease as would be expected in a person with Down syndrome (where Alzheimer's can move more quickly). Recently Matt has had a couple of incidents that raise those red flags, but for now it appears that final good-bye has been delayed.

I have had to let go of some of our connections, however. We used to have Matt visit several times a year and those visits included staying with us overnight. Matt now needs to have a consistent routine so sleep-overs at Mom's don't happen any longer. Thanksgiving and Christmas with the entire family are sometimes too stimulating for Matt and after just a few hours he begins to show signs of agitation. Letting go of our family traditions that included Matt has been difficult. I am grateful though that we can at least have short periods to celebrate with him.

I have always been the lead when decisions needed to be made about Matt's life. However, as I grow older by the calendar, I

feel I still have much to do in my life. I want to spend the years I have left being Matt's old and wonderful Momma, so months before Joe's final illness and death, we made the difficult decision to let go of our legal responsibility to Matt. We embarked on the process to have our friend, Michelle Dean, appointed as Matt's Guardian Advocate. She is the perfect person to do this job as she has known Matt for more than twenty years and is like a daughter to me. I trust her to do her very best to give him the life he deserves. I am confident that I will be able to enjoy visits with Matt, without the worry of whether he has his doctor appointments scheduled or if he has enough money for his rent and groceries.

Letting go has been an incredible gift that surprised me when I found it so many years ago. But, letting go is a release and I'm ready to peek into that gift box whenever I need to. I'm ready to rest in that sense of calm and security that letting go has brought me. Matt's butterfly eyelash kisses, big strong, heartfelt hugs, and his sign for "I love you" will be the best reward of this gift of letting go.

Letting go can:

- Create opportunities for new dreams.

- Allow for more growth.

- Bring peace and serenity to a troubled heart.

My Gift to You

In my final gift to you, I hope that you see the wonder in letting go in your life. It is freeing to allow the things that need to move on or disappear to just be finished. I appreciate that letting go isn't always easy— in fact some things are very difficult to release.

1. Think about something that you have let go of, and with its release, you found a sense of relief. It may be a responsibility, an obligation, or feelings. Write about it below.

   _____

   _____

   _____

2. How can you know when it's time to let go?

   _____

   _____

   _____

3. Is there something you need to let go of, that you aren't sure you are ready to release? What would help you let go?

_____

_____

_____

DEAR MATT:
ANYTHING IS POSSIBLE

Dear Matt,

Telling our story through the gifts I have received has been such fun for me, my precious and wonderful son. I recently read an article about personal empowerment that seemed to tie together the life that we have shared.

I end our story with the hope that you recognize the empowered life you live. You are one who has, very quietly (and sometimes not so quietly), brought about some incredible changes in the Down syndrome world just because you are in it. Your life led me to learn, and to grow. As I have shared the lessons you taught me, I have been able to help other families who walk the path beside us and behind us.

Opportunities have been created because you helped me realize that anything is possible.

Anything is possible when I have the right attitude. Matt, your beautiful smile reminds me to see the good in life.

Anything is possible when I find contentment in being who I am. How clearly you have demonstrated that living life on your terms is what is important. You have never measured your success against the success of others—something, I have been guilty of. As I watched you, I have found comfort as I learned to live my life in the same way.

Anything is possible when I trust that I have the strength and power to get the hard stuff done, and when I remember that the hard stuff doesn't last. You led me, over and over, through some really tough times and eventually I learned that my strength would pull me to the other side. And that strengthens the hopefulness you taught me.

Anything is possible when I face life's challenges with grace—when I do what I love and love what I do.

Matt, you have taught me all of this and your teaching touches people you have never met. Your life has had a positive influence on me, on those around you, and those who only know you through your stories. Keep living your incredible life, teaching all of us about what is important. Keep loving the way you do, with all your being. Keep smiling—it endears those who get to be with you. And most of all, Matt, keep laughing. Your laughter raises my spirits and helps me know that life is still fun.

Matt, thank you for choosing me to be your student, and more importantly, for choosing me to be your mom.

All My Love and Admiration,
Momma

ABOUT THE AUTHOR

J adene Sloan Ransdell has a B.S. in Special Education and nearly fifty years of experience working with families and professionals in many areas related to developmental disabilities.

Jadene's knowledge of family and disability issues is enhanced by her first-hand life adventures with her own family. She and her husband, Joe, shared 51 years together before his death from COVID in March 2021. Their older son, Michael, is a single father with two sons. Jadene's and Joe's younger son, Matthew, was born with Down syndrome, and has additional diagnoses of Autism, and Apraxia. Despite a more recent diagnosis of Alzheimer's disease, Matt still leads a successful life of his own, with supports in the community. Jadene's real-world experiences with Matt bring a unique perspective to her work which she shares through her writing, workshops, and seminars.

Jadene's skills include public speaking, creative writing, product development and conference planning. She has worked with state-wide education systems and developmental disabilities agencies in several states, and in public school classrooms as well as family involvement programs. Her background also includes the administration of local community, state, and federal programs serving families—including military families who had children with disabilities living in Germany.

Her work as a family advocate led her to serve as a volunteer on numerous boards, councils, and organizations. She is a lifetime member of the Family Network on Disabilities of Florida and was a member of the 1998 class of Florida's Partners in Policymaking. As a former consultant and staff member to the National Down Syndrome Society, Jadene created a national conference focused on adults with Down syndrome, the first of its kind in the United States. Later, she helped develop their Aging and Caregiving programs. A former board member of the National Task Group on Intellectual Disabilities and Dementia Practices, Jadene served as the co-chair of the Family Support and Advocacy committee, co-facilitated their national, web-based family caregiver support group, and authored a quarterly caregiver newsletter that was disseminated worldwide. In addition, she administers a Down syndrome and Alzheimer's Facebook group that supports nearly 1,000 members in the United States and around the world.

Jadene has been the recipient of many awards and recognitions throughout her career.

> ➢ ***Stephen Beck, Jr. Award, Champion of Change***
> 2019, National Down Syndrome Society, Washington, DC

- ***Spirit of the NTG Award***
  2017, National Task Group on Intellectual Disabilities and Dementia Practices (NTG), Houston, Texas

- ***Award of Appreciation***
  1986, U. S. Forces Police, U.S. Air Force, Kaiserslautern, Germany

- ***3,000 Hour Volunteer Recognition Award***
  1985, 21st Support Command, U.S. Army, Kaiserslautern, Germany

- ***Great American Family Award***
  1984, 29th Area Support Group, U.S. Army, Kaiserslautern, Germany

- ***Outstanding Special Education Graduate***
  1980, Columbus College, Columbus, Georgia

In addition to her book, *Unwrapping the Gifts of Disability: A Mother's Reflections on Raising a Son with Down Syndrome,* Jadene began a blog shortly after Matt was diagnosed with Alzheimer's to share the challenges and joys encountered by families and people with Down syndrome who are over 40.

Jadene can be reached through her website (www.agingwithdownsyndrome.com) or at jadene@agingwithdownsyndrome.com

ACKNOWLEDGMENTS

When I was a little girl, living in Iowa, my grandmother, Echo Sloan, bribed me with a quarter for every letter I wrote to her when she retired to Florida. She also taught me the importance of writing a personal thank you note for any gifts I received. I suppose since this book is a story filled with gifts, it is fitting that I write a thank you note to every person who helped me get this story in print.

My beloved husband, Joe, you were the first to support my dream to write, and you gently pushed me to return to the keyboard whenever I stopped writing for too long. You patiently listened as I read and reread my stories and loved me through their telling. I am so sorry I wasn't quick enough for you to see this book in print.

Matt, dear Matt, there would be no story to share without you, my son. Your birth changed the direction of my life—you filled it with meaning, you encouraged me to grow and learn, and you helped me to feel deeply. Matt, I am a better person because I share my life with you.

Dear Michael, you were the one person who kept me grounded and helped me see the world through a boy's eyes. As my first born, Michael, you gently led me to give Matt space to be himself and challenged me to push him when the time was right. You always seemed to know when that was. Thank you Michael for being a son and brother who taught me that different is not less than.

Dear Doug Mantooth, thank you for teaching Matt and me so many years ago. You were a young educator who was very wise in your approach to a troubled student and a mom who doubted her own abilities. It feels like a lifetime ago that we met, and a lifetime since we've been together, yet that friendship sustained me through many difficult days. I've often read that we may never know whose lives we have touched; I hope you know that your words helped me find the strength to persevere at one of the darkest times in my life and many times thereafter.

Dear Lizzie Sloan—Beth, as you will always be known to me—thank you for helping me pull this book from deep inside where it was hidden for decades. You held my hand, were so gentle with my heart and encouraged me to just write. Without you, this story would still be in my head.

Dear Linda Bendorf, Blue Sage Writing, and fellow writers in the memoir workshops, I found my writing voice in those workshops and received amazing constructive criticism from all of you, my writing pals. Becca King, Constance Frank, Faith Trapp, Gloria Mallory, John Bos, Lee Anne Willson, Linda Young, Lindsay Hill, Lynn Alex, Norma Wolff, and Richard Potter: thank you for your kind words and powerful suggestions. The connection we share helped me improve with every story.

Dear Jaren Sloan-Levy, Doug Mantooth, Becca King, Paula Petry, and Embry Burris, your feedback, as readers of early drafts of this book, is valued and appreciated. Each of you read this story from the way you know Matt and me. That provided the perfect mix of insight for many excellent improvements.

Acknowledgments

My dear Will Schermerhorn, editor extraordinaire, thank you for the hours you pored over my story; you brought it from good to amazing. Your ideas, guidance, and support have moved this manuscript to be its best.

Dear Ultimate World Publishing team, I give thanks to you all for showing up when I was overwhelmed with all the steps I needed to take to get this book in print. I am grateful to my friend, Julie Fisher for opening the door, to Natasa and Stuart Denman for the brilliant business they run helping first time authors, Marinda Wilkinson for the final edits that brought this work to a piece that I am so very proud of, and the amazing team behind the scenes who helped me polish this book and get it in the hands of readers.

NOTES

_____

_____

_____

_____

_____

_____

_____

_____

_____

_____

_____

_____

CPSIA information can be obtained
at www.ICGtesting.com
Printed in the USA
JSHW010222180323
39062JS00004B/12